THE
ALASTAIR COOK
STORY

BY OLIVER BRETT

© SJH Publishing 2019

First edition

Published by SJH Publishing

298 Regents Park Road, London N3 2SZ

020 8371 4000

sjhpublishing.org

ISBN: 978-1-906670-81-8

Printed and bound in the UK by CPI Books.

FOR MY SON LUKE, WHO WILL BE A VERY FINE CRICKETER ONCE HE
SHOWS A LITTLE OF THE PATIENCE OF SIR ALASTAIR COOK

Oliver Brett fell in love with cricket when taken, as an eight-year-old, to the famous Headingley Ashes Test of 1981. He began his journalism career at the *Grimsby Evening Telegraph* in the 1990s and then spent 10 years as a cricket reporter for BBC Sport Online before stepping into freelance territory. As well as cricket, he writes on horse racing and tennis. *The Alastair Cook Story* is his first book.

CONTENTS

FOREWORD 7

INTRODUCTION 11

CHAPTER ONE BEGINNINGS – GARDEN CRICKET.............................19

CHAPTER TWO BEDDING IN 24

CHAPTER THREE BREAKING THROUGH 41

CHAPTER FOUR A HURRIED TEST DEBUT 54

CHAPTER FIVE HOME COMFORTS AND TEST CENTURIES 64

CHAPTER SIX THE ASHES – A RUDE AWAKENING 73

CHAPTER SEVEN INTERNATIONAL CREDENTIALS 79

CHAPTER EIGHT TURMOIL AT THE TOP 93

CHAPTER NINE THE ASHES RECLAIMED 107

CHAPTER TEN A TASTE OF THE CAPTAINCY 119

CHAPTER ELEVEN RUNS IN AUSTRALIA 124

CHAPTER TWELVE THE ONE-DAY CAPTAINCY 145

CHAPTER THIRTEEN PIETERSEN, STRAUSS, AND
THE TEST CAPTAINCY 160

CHAPTER FOURTEEN SUCCESS IN INDIA 170

CHAPTER FIFTEEN CHAMPIONS TROPHY AGONY 181

CHAPTER SIXTEEN PERSONAL FRUSTRATIONS 190

CHAPTER SEVENTEEN MAJOR SERIES SUCCESSES 205

CHAPTER EIGHTEEN RETURNING TO ESSEX 217

CHAPTER NINETEEN THE PERFECT SEND-OFF 223

FOREWORD

BY DANIEL NORCROSS, TEST MATCH SPECIAL

At 12.45pm on 9 September 2018 an avalanche of noise engulfed the Kennington Oval. It began as an exultant roar, born of relief at the resolution of an unbearably tense moment. But the sound would morph and grow. Relief would give way to admiration, which in turn transformed into something I'd never heard before at a cricket ground. It was, I'm pretty certain, the giant collective gratitude of a sporting nation. The recipient of this unique paean looked hugely embarrassed. He diffidently raised his bat to all parts of the crowd, but the noise was only getting louder. He prodded the pitch. He looked at the umpire apologetically, as if to say, 'I can't make it stop.' As we entered the third minute of this unprecedented tenth standing ovation of the match, I started to wonder – on commentary in the *Test Match Special* box – if the players should just take lunch twelve minutes early. Eventually, the noise dampened down and became a loud murmur of delight; laughter mixed with incredulity at what we had all witnessed. The perfect end to a career that will, in its own right, come to define twelve years of England's cricketing history.

The symmetry of Alastair Cook's Test career – starting with a fifty and a hundred against India at Nagpur, and ending with a fifty and a hundred against the same opponents at the Oval – seems, with the benefit of hindsight, to have been inevitable. He was a man so neat, so controlled, so selfless that he could even tidy up his statistics for us. Like the dream employee who, on retirement, has left no issue unresolved, has emptied his desk, and even gone to the bother of cleaning his keyboard and monitor.

Cook's career wasn't always plain sailing, of course, and he wasn't always universally appreciated in England. Naturally, he had ups and downs in form. Before his career-defining tour of Australia in 2010–11 he'd been tied in knots by Pakistan's seamers but, in an almost premonitory fashion that foreshadowed his ultimate farewell century, he eked out a beleaguered hundred at the Oval with the help of four overthrows in the final Test of the summer.

Many fans unfairly resented him for being described by Giles Clarke, then Chairman of the England and Wales Cricket Board (ECB), as being from 'the right sort of family'. His limited stroke play and approach to the discipline of batting seemed to be shrouded in recherché qualities that had been going out of fashion even before his career began. He avoided social media, frequently appeared stilted in interviews, and probably emptied his first bar during his last Test innings.

So how did he come to induce the collective outpouring of love that final time at the Oval? A love that made you feel like you were at a wake for a beloved relative.

It was, in part, because of those recherché qualities. His conspicuous refusal to engage in self-promotion was rare in the modern age. His discomfort with the media perversely connected him to thousands of fans who recognised in him something of themselves. His self-denial in playing only the shots he was confident he could execute. His willingness to march out against the best new-ball bowlers in the world for twelve years and perform the hardest task that cricket, in any of its formats, has to offer.

Unlike Jos Buttler or Ben Stokes, who are tasked with inspiring the younger generation and dragging cricket out of its (largely imagined) doldrums, Cook was a player about whom you simply asked, 'Is he still in?' Because if he was still in, all was safe and secure and comforting. You didn't need to *watch* him being in. In fact, it was frequently better not to undergo the torment of witnessing his cussed struggles with his off stump, his stiff legs, his head falling over. You could clean the bathroom. You could visit your in-laws. You could fill in your tax return. And on top of it all, you sensed that he was happy for you to get on with your life while he took on the challenge of upholding England's dignity on our behalf.

Perhaps the most important of his qualities was his durability; his ever-presence. He played 159 consecutive Test matches. For those twelve years he, more even than Jimmy Anderson and Stuart Broad, lived the story – the history of English cricket. I am not alone in marking where I was and what I was doing in reference to Cook's career from the moment he stepped out that first time in Nagpur. His career holds almost Proustian resonances for generations of cricket fans. I can almost taste the bout of Norovirus that afflicted me whenever I recall Cook and Strauss batting Australia out of the Melbourne Test on that Boxing Day in 2010. I can recreate with perfect clarity the rooms I was in, food I was eating, the positions of the beer cans on the side tables when he scored his hundreds against India in 2012. His life was, somehow, our lives, and with his retirement we had to acknowledge that we too were mortal. Careers end. Lives end. That day at the Oval truly was a wake but, uniquely, it was a wake not just for a living man, but for an era that all cricket fans shared.

And it was tinged with the very real fear that we will not ever again witness a player like Alastair Cook.

INTRODUCTION

THE SUMMER OF ALL SUMMERS

The 2005 Ashes series was probably the most epic and unforgettable Test series of all time. It started at Lord's on 21 July with one extraordinary day of turbulent fortunes for both teams, and ended on 12 September at the Oval with scenes of stomach-churning panic at lunch, before the glorious release of joyful celebration at the end. (Unless you were Australian.)

In between, there were two desperately tight finishes in Birmingham and Manchester, and a match at Nottingham that in any ordinary year would have been regarded as a classic in its own right. Something changed that summer: a collection of cricketers who could have previously popped into their local corner shop unrecognised by most passers-by had become superstars. In England, cricketers are very rarely superstars.

England's glorious gladiators were paraded on an open-top bus across central London. They had beaten the old enemy Australia in a saga that had occupied the hearts and minds of so many people for weeks. Strange things happened that never happen in cricket during the series. Fans travelled hundreds of miles with slim hopes of securing tickets simply to be in the vicinity of a historic sporting drama. Some of it made sense. No England supporter under the age of thirty had seen an Ashes win before. It hadn't happened since Margaret Thatcher was in her prime, the Communards were big in the charts, and British Gas floated on the stock exchange.

In 2005, many of the fans jostling for space in Trafalgar Square to catch a glimpse of Hoggy or Straussy or Tres had never heard of the Communards. They were there on a cloudless early autumn morning queuing up to cheer the gifted Kevin Pietersen and his ludicrous 'dead skunk' haircut, and Andrew 'Freddie' Flintoff too, of course, whose bleary eyes and happily hungover demeanour betrayed the overwhelming volume of refreshments consumed during the previous night of partying.

Every single player in the team – even Paul Collingwood who came in for the finale at the expense of the injured Simon Jones – was appointed an MBE. The coach, Duncan Fletcher, and the Chairman of Selectors, David Graveney, received OBEs.

Cricket had been elevated on to front pages that summer, and the established fans, the new fans, the old fans, the young ones, pretty much everybody, or so it seemed, watched it all unfold. Every nuance, agonising or triumphal, was played out in front of thousands around the country on free-to-air television.

Nobody since has been able to watch England play cricket live on television without paying a premium to do so. The grass-roots game is struggling, with coaches at some well-established clubs finding it hard to recruit sustainable numbers of players at junior levels.

In 2020, a handful of matches (mainly domestic but including two men's Twenty20 internationals) will be shown on the BBC in what might herald the start of a new era of accessibility. If so, that will signal the end of a fifteen-year period in which the English game has survived, to some extent, rather than thrived, starved of the oxygen provided by terrestrial television in an age of so many conflicting and competing interests.

It is also a fifteen-year period which, it so happens, has produced the career of one of the best batsmen England have ever produced, but a man who, quite unlike Pietersen or Flintoff in 2005, could probably pop out to buy a pint of milk without being besieged with selfie requests. That man is, of course, Sir Alastair Cook, the subject of this book, and the holder of a great swathe of national batting records. On 26 February 2019, he became the first

England cricketer to receive a knighthood since Sir Ian Botham in 2007, and the first *active* one since New Zealand's gifted fast bowler Sir Richard Hadlee in 1990.

He is active in the sense that he is still employed to play professional cricket. But, as of now, his cheques will be signed by the Chief Executive of Essex County Cricket Club rather than the England and Wales Cricket Board.

Cook retired from Tests aged thirty-three in September 2018. He had played in 160 Test matches, but gave himself one more, against India. In seven innings across the first four Tests he had failed to reach thirty once, and the fire was not burning as brightly inside as it once had.

'There's nothing left in the tank,' he said in an official statement that had an unusually personal tone. And yet, somewhat theatrically, he gave himself the perfect send-off. With the burden of expectation released, with nothing to fear in terms of ensuring his place on England's winter tours, he signed off with scores of 71 and 147. Twelve years earlier, making a surprise and rushed debut against the same opponents in Nagpur, he had accumulated scores of 60 and 104 not out. An outstanding career bookended by centuries against India – a most satisfactory conclusion.

There was more than a tinge of surprise that Cook was giving it all up, even so. He has always been one of the fittest players in the squad. At thirty-three, you are considered somewhere around your prime as a batsman in modern cricket. Chris Gayle is still the most important member of the West Indies one-day side and he's thirty-nine (although considerably less mobile than he once was). But after those four disappointing Tests in 2018, Cook felt it was the right time to call time. The 'nothing left in the tank' comment was refreshingly candid. The feeling he had occupied the bubble for long enough was stronger than the desire to break even more records. Not everyone felt charitable about this turn of events at the fag end of an unusually long, hot summer. David 'Bumble' Lloyd, the popular Sky Sports commentator, opined that the England management should not have allowed Cook the chance of playing in that final Test at all.

One theme of this book will be to explore the underappreciation of Alastair Cook among his own compatriots. I have already alluded to the fact that a game with the subtle complexities of cricket has not been helped by being broadcast exclusively on paid-for networks for such a long time. In addition, Cook is also the last person in professional sport you would expect to actively seek the limelight. He has no interest in social media, celebrity photo opportunities and the like. For twelve and a half years he did his thing, which was to score lots of runs for his country and in so doing try to help them win as many Test matches as possible. In between times, he escaped to the working farm near Leighton Buzzard that he still maintains with his wife, Alice. He was once asked in an interview if he had ever had posters of celebrities on his bedroom wall growing up. 'No. Just wallpaper,' was the curt answer.

You may or may not be aware of the television quiz show *Pointless*, in which a hundred members of the public are asked various questions of factual trivia, and contestants must find correct answers that are given by as few participants from the pool of a hundred as possible.

In one such episode from February 2018, the following question was posed: name the England cricketer who in 2016 became the youngest player to score ten thousand Test runs. The initials AC in brackets followed the question, just to make things a little easier.

Only nineteen of the hundred were able to supply the answer Alastair Cook. There were several questions on the same survey which people found significantly easier. A quarter of the hundred individuals knew that the British explorer who completed a surface circumnavigation of the globe by both poles in 1982 was Ranulph Fiennes, and forty-two were able to give Paula Radcliffe as the British runner who broke the women's world record at the 2003 London Marathon. Just under half knew Roger Bannister had run a sub-four-minute mile in 1954, while sixty-four could name Richard Branson as the businessman who crossed the Atlantic in a hot air balloon in 1987.

The relevance of all this is that it tends to suggest two things. One is that Cook's remarkable and often heroic sporting pursuits have not resonated as strongly as they have deserved to. But there is, of course, another: cricket, while retaining an ardent core of diehard aficionados, as almost every leisure pursuit has done generation after generation, does not stir the masses as we head towards the third decade of the twenty-first century. The advent of Twenty20 has provided a commercial uplift and helped sustain a wider demographic of support, but the sport has lost that special connection it had with the British public in the heady summer of 2005. If Cook had been a little more like Pietersen – the arch-showman, the entertainer, the controversy magnet; indeed, Cook's very antithesis – one suspects more than nineteen of the hundred individuals panelled by *Pointless* would have identified Cook as the answer to that question. Nobody, however, is under the illusion that cricket can continue to be regarded as the summer cousin of football as it once was in the national consciousness.

Back in 2005, while attentions were firmly focused on the drama involving the national side, a young Alastair Cook was enjoying something of a breakthrough year too. He was the top scorer for his county, Essex, in first-class cricket with 1,249 runs – quite an achievement given the presence of Andy Flower and Ronnie Irani on the staff, two experienced and talented operators. Cook, aged twenty, was in his first full season for the club.

When the Ashes were on and Essex were playing, the members' attentions were not always where they should have been. Cook recalls in his autobiography *Starting Out – My Story So Far*, 'When we were warming up for a game against Middlesex, all the spectators were congregated at one end of the ground, watching the climax of the Edgbaston Test on a television. A huge cheer went up when Michael Kasprowicz was out and England had won, certainly far bigger than anything that was heard during our game later that day! It felt good to be a cricketer, a proud time for the game.'

There was one stand-out innings from the youngster that season which still resonates. It just so happened that it was compiled against the Australians in their final county warm-up match. 'Essex opener Alastair Cook ruined Australia's build-up to the final Test with a blazing 214 in their tour match,' reported the BBC Sport website on the evening of 3 September after a day in which the county had racked up an extraordinary 502-4.

Cook needed just forty-nine balls to bring up his half-century, and 107 to go through to three figures. It was the worst possible preparation for bowlers like Brett Lee and Jason Gillespie as they looked for some confidence-boosting form against a Division Two county side.

A day after being named England's Young Cricketer of the Year, Cook took three boundaries in Brett Lee's second over. The tall blond paceman was among the most fearsome of fast bowlers of that era. In the self-effacing manner that would characterise his future dealings with the media, he brushed off any suggestions that he had done something special against the best team in the world.

'Flat track ... things went my way ... you have to make the most of little bits of good fortune.' Cook was almost apologetic about ripping the Aussie attack to shreds. There was no place yet for him in an England team which was about to beat Australia in a Test series for the first time since 1986–87. It would come though, and as circumstances developed, it came a fair bit sooner than he expected.

CHAPTER ONE

BEGINNINGS – GARDEN CRICKET

The middle of three boys, Alastair Cook was born on Christmas Day 1984, two months premature, to Graham and Stephanie, and grew up in the Essex village of Wickham Bishops. It is an unremarkable sort of place, with a church, a village hall, a library and a hair salon. Its pub was for many years simply a typical English country boozer with cask beer and unpretentious food like gammon and eggs on the menu. It has recently been tarted up and turned into a restaurant, serving upmarket Italian food at London prices. Children under the age of ten are not permitted on Friday and Saturday evenings, and customers are advised to 'embrace a smart/casual dress code'. Hoodies, tracksuits and sports shorts are expressly forbidden.

Regular activities provided at a smart village hall built in 2006 include Brownies, bridge, and wine-tasting. It has adjoining tennis courts. Some two thousand people live there and some of the grander family homes are on the market for more than a million pounds. However, there is a proliferation of more modest two-storey homes with garages. They look like they were probably built in the post-war era.

Wickham Bishops was probably slightly different in the eighties and nineties when Alastair Cook was growing up there. Among his earliest memories are playing fiercely competitive games of cricket in the garden of the family home with his two brothers, Adrian and Laurence.

At a mere eleven yards, the pitch was half the 'correct' length for an adult wicket, and older brother Adrian bowled fast and short, thankfully with a plastic ball, but a painful one all the same if it hit the young Alastair on an unprotected part of his body.

Anyone who has played garden cricket will know that a highly unpredictable, uneven bounce is one of the hazards you have to accept as a batsman; the principal advantage of staying at the crease, however, is to watch your siblings or parents tire in their efforts to dismiss you, and perhaps the biggest incentive of all is to stop anyone else from having a bat.

For a tall man exposed to the best fast bowling in the world, the adult Alastair Cook was a fine player of short-pitched bowling and to this day he credits his success in this realm to that half-length wicket on which Adrian would bowl him bouncer after bouncer in a bid to unsettle his brother. Poor Laurence had to spend most of the time observing this duel as the solitary fielder, before often wandering off altogether in eventual boredom.

Alastair, however, was not hitting Adrian over the garden wall with any regularity. He did not learn the pull shot, the staple attacking option for a batsman to utilise when repelling short-pitched bowling, until he was fourteen and in his first summer at Bedford School.

However, what he *did* learn was how to sway inside the line, duck, and deflect the ball safely away. He learned to avoid getting out, making use of the God-given hand-eye coordination he had, and was blessed with survival instincts and a fiercely if quietly competitive streak that would stand him in good stead through every stage of his playing career.

The games with Adrian and Laurence would start soon after breakfast and continue most of the day if the weather was fine. It was not purely a cricket diet either – football, rugby, tennis and badminton were added to the mix. None of the three brothers craved a PlayStation – they had each other and the visceral appeal of real support.

The Cook parents played tennis and golf to a high level, and they were also both involved in cricket. Stephanie, the daughter of a Welsh steelworker, who was a teacher, scored at the cricket club at Great Totham, the adjoining village to Wickham Bishops. Graham, who spent his weekdays as a BT engineer, was one of the best batsmen in the team.

In the next chapter, you will hear how Mr and Mrs Cook were admired by the Bedford School teaching fraternity as model parents. The first glimpses of their superior skills in this regard came in their gentle insistence that music, as well as sport, had to play its part in the formative years for the three Cook boys.

Alastair took lessons on the recorder – he would later play the clarinet – and had to spend many hours practising, though his chief musical vocation was his voice and he was booked into the Wickham Bishops choir for practice on Friday evenings, before singing alongside the rest of the choir through the various Sunday services. His mother was also in the choir so there was no question of him bunking off, though one doubts he would have been that way inclined.

One evening, the local choirmaster persuaded Stephanie and Graham to take Alastair to St Paul's Cathedral School. It took just one song, delivered with precision by the presumably angelic voice of an eight-year-old boy, to earn a place at one of the most sought-after choir schools in the world.

The downside was that he would have to board, and stay over at weekends because the weekly rhythm of a choir school dictated that performances were delivered at the end of the week to coincide with Sunday services.

Graham and Stephanie's weekends now involved regular commutes to central London to catch a glimpse of their small son who suffered from homesickness in what was an alien environment – even the sound of traffic passing at night was a novelty to a boy who knew of little outside rural Essex.

The regimental timetable, with two hours of singing practice every day shoehorned between lessons, mealtimes and homework, meant the pupils were on the go from 7am to 9pm every night. Weekends had no lessons, but even more singing and, of course, services. It sounds exhausting. There is no suggestion that Cook found it a terrible chore, just the feeling that he was not as happy at St Paul's as he had been beforehand at home, and certainly not as happy as he would be at Bedford. The discipline and high expectations of choir school probably helped him in his cricket; Graham Cook goes further, to assert that his middle son would not have had a successful international career in cricket without those five years at St Paul's.

That said, every year the highlight of Cook's year was the start of the summer holidays, and every year its low point was September, and the journey back to London to start another academic year.

St Paul's did allow some time for sport, and Cook scored a hundred against Westminster Abbey. He was also allowed to play for London schools and scored what he has called his first 'proper' hundred against Berkshire.

At an Under-12 tournament, he met his exact contemporary Ravi Bopara, a future Essex and England teammate at various age-group levels – though on this rare occasion they were on opposing sides. This would have probably been 1997 – and in the summer of 2019, some twenty-two years on, both are still playing for Essex now, their England days behind them but the competitive desire still burning bright.

CHAPTER TWO

BEDDING IN

Felsted School would have been a likely option for Alastair Cook's next school. Essex and England cricketers such as Derek Pringle and John Stephenson had spent their formative years there and, having not entirely fallen in love with boarding, Cook would have had the option of living at home once again.

However, the parents of a friend recommended Bedford instead. A boys-only boarding school, Bedford had – and still has – a reputation for allowing its students to flourish across multiple endeavours, be it sport, music, drama or academic studies.

A music scholarship which knocked off a good percentage of the fees was obtained, and Cook, an inch or three shorter than a typical thirteen-year-old boy, was sent to a boarding house off-site that tended to be frequented by the more gifted athletes in the school.

Bedford were well aware of Cook's burgeoning sporting ability, and though his music scholarship meant he had to spend time on the clarinet and with the choir, the philosophy was to give him access to multiple pursuits rather than apply restrictions.

Jeremy Farrell, now deputy head at Sutton Valence, a mixed school in Kent, was the master in charge of cricket at Bedford at the time, and even before the summer term started in anger, there was a frisson of excitement about the cricketing talent exhibited by this diminutive Essex-based chorister.

It took just one session with then coach Andy Pick, a former first-class cricketer of some distinction who is now Nottinghamshire's bowling coach, to understand that the name A. Cook would feature prominently in Bedford scorecards for many a year.

'Alastair was tiny, absolutely tiny,' recalls Farrell. 'We knew a little bit about him and he had a net with Andy, and Andy told me he was very excited. With Alastair at that stage it was all about placement, and deflecting the ball, using the pace on offer. Sometimes in a net against a bowling machine you can understand a lot about a young cricketer and you could see straight away there was somebody who was determined to make the most of everything he had.'

A few considerations now came into play. The first was to manage Cook's own expectations. He had eyes on the First XI straight away, but that would involve playing alongside and against eighteen-year-olds. Cook was a fourteen-year-old who looked two years younger and hadn't started his growth spurt.

Then there was the music. It would have been irresponsible for the PE department to ignore the fact that Cook was there as a music scholar. In fact, Andrew Morris, the head of music, wouldn't have conceded any ground in this regard, by all accounts.

As Barry Burgess – now the director of sport at Bedford who, back then, specialised in rugby – recalls, Farrell and Morris would have both worked hard to get the most out of Alastair, while putting the young man's own needs at the top of their list of priorities.

'Andrew would have been pretty determined and pretty vociferous in making music scholars do what they had to do. I'd be amazed if he didn't do what he had to do in music.

'Schools are used to having students who excel in different areas, and they tend to dovetail rather than fight against each other – there are ways of making boys excel in a number of different areas without being pulled from pillar to post.

'I think that's how it would have worked for Cooky when he was here because Jeremy and Andrew were both pretty fierce characters who would have been opinionated about what was going on.'

For a variety of reasons, Farrell resisted the temptation to plunge Cook straight into the First XI when the matches began. Cook, who loved everything else that Bedford had provided him up to then, was upset about it. He felt he had the tools required to warrant a place in the First XI.

The first few matches came with Cook scoring big runs for the Under-14 team and watching with envy the exploits of those at the top of the school.

Farrell explains: 'We had quite a good record of doing things the right way at the right time. I was keen to build a foundation so you had a quality provision, a pathway if you like. Generally, boys played Under-14s, Under-15s, Under-16s, second team and then you could get into the first team in your last year. But equally I wanted people to play at the right level at the right time. In some schools, the best eleven players were automatically picked and you would end up with a really talented boy batting at seven, doing a lot of fielding but not getting to do a lot of batting. I wanted to give the bloke who had followed the pathway his chance, and that meant I was giving Alastair a chance to earn his spurs.'

However, divine providence arrived in the shape of a visiting Marylebone Cricket Club (MCC) team who were missing a player. Somebody had to be 'lent' to the opposition – and Cook was the candidate for the unexpected call-up.

Farrell says: 'We got lucky! He came into that match, not exactly kicking and screaming because I pulled him out of double physics lesson. He batted number three. The beauty of it is that in 1999 the thought of clearing the infield is not what you were working on with the players. And facing older, fast bowlers helped him play better because there was more pace on the ball and he could play it off the back foot, nudge it here and there …

the number of eighteen-year-olds who saw this little squit and thought they could bounce him out – well, he would just say "Fine, thanks. I'll tuck you here, I'll tuck you there."'

Tucking them here and there he did – pouring the misery on his own schoolmates, most of whom were four years older than him and twice his size. He scored a century, reaching the landmark with an uncharacteristically bold strike, lofting a ball high over the midwicket's head for four. Cook has called his attitude during this whole episode 'very stubborn' and has even stated he was 'probably a bit arrogant in my belief in my ability'.

Burgess explains: 'Someone of that level playing first-team cricket, even four years younger than most of the other players, would look pretty comfortable. You've got to be mindful of the whole social element of playing in different groups. It can be quite a big deal but cricket is pretty much the only sport where that happens as a matter of course and it's good because you need to stretch the boys who have the potential to be professional cricketers. It would be too easy for them just playing in their own year group. And in terms of the level someone like Cooky would have been playing at he would have warranted being in the first team. But in other sports that doesn't happen. Rugby, hockey and other sports don't lend themselves to that.'

Farrell took the innings as his cue to elevate Cook to the First XI permanently. In reality, he probably had no other option. It meant James Degroot being dropped to the seconds. 'Dear old James,' says Farrell. 'He'd earned his time but I had to sit on the bench with him outside the dining hall at Bedford and tell him he'd had three or four chances, it hadn't really worked and it was time for someone else to have a go. James now works in the catering staff at Lord's.'

Cook's first innings opening the batting for the school came with instructions. Farrell told him to concentrate on staying at the crease, not to attempt anything elaborate – and he'd only got to twenty-five at lunch. Afterwards, as he so often did, he began to accelerate his scoring effortlessly as the ball got softer and bowlers more tired.

Bedford still kept Cook's progress in check. Farrell remembers: 'It was about managing him to make sure he didn't overstretch himself. In the second year he did a bit of wicketkeeping and we had to start thinking about whether he would open the batting if we fielded first because in those days in school cricket you could end up fielding for seventy-five overs. There were a few times we had to give him time to rest or play in his own peer group in Cup games.'

What was Cook like as a character? 'Very self-contained – and that's one of the things many people will have noticed. You have these schoolboy stars and undoubtedly in his time he was one of the best schoolboy sportsmen in the country, and some don't win the approval of the opposition. You see this a little bit with someone like Virat Kohli. Alastair was quite the opposite – no real ego, absolutely trying to win and driving himself, but not at all costs.'

Burgess and Farrell are in agreement that Cook was neither arrogant nor stubborn around this time. They do agree that he was exceptionally determined, however, and that his parents were absolute role models of how parents should behave when watching their children compete.

Farrell says: 'Alastair should really do a parenting seminar some time – they were just so unobtrusive, sitting in the pavilion every Saturday, not seeming to care about whether he got a hundred or nought, not putting pressure on him to go out and perform and equally supportive of his younger brother Laurence.

'One of the real concerns in all sports is that moment when somebody finds themselves playing for more than just the enjoyment of the game and themselves. And it's all about body language. The Cooks were very undemonstrative. There was never any "Here we are, look – we're the captain of the XI's parents." They just had a very gentle manner and were not looking to draw attention to themselves in any shape or form. They wanted to split their free time equally between the three boys.'

By contrast, plenty of school parents behave quite shamelessly in these situations. Farrell has had to approach parents: 'Please, just let him or her play.' The worst scenario is that you run the risk of putting them off sport for ever.

As Cook continued to excel in the Bedford First XI, constant dialogue was maintained between the school and Essex, who by now were keen to take a stake in his development and yet relaxed enough to allow him to develop his game at the school, at least during term time. Then there was Derek Randall, who was the Bedford coach from the start of Cook's third year of five in the first team. A complex, slightly wacky and somewhat disorganised individual, Randall had been good enough to play forty-seven Tests for England and hit an outstanding 174 in the Centenary Test at the Melbourne Cricket Ground (MCG) in 1977.

Randall had a natural affinity when it came to working on Cook's batting, and Farrell suspects it may have been because his own potential was not quite realised as an international cricketer.

'Andy Pick was brilliant on the team thing; Richard Bates, who came to us for a year, was a very good technician; and then there was Derek. And with Derek there was an element of the maverick. But there was modesty too, and he knew what it took to score runs. During Derek's playing career, at times people had tried to change him too much and that was the worst thing that could have happened to him and I think he was quite a thoughtful coach. Although a bit zany at times, he consciously thought about how little he could get away with in terms of changing someone while also getting the most out of them.

'These players get all sorts of people offering them advice. Alastair was very good at looking someone in the eye, nodding and saying the right things and then leaving the room and it all went out of his mind, whereas others would probably try and experiment a bit, give it a go. Even then, aged fourteen or fifteen, he knew in his own mind what his own game was. He knew the things he could do and the things he couldn't. It was as simple as that. Learning to play the pull shot was a key thing for him, because once he began pulling the ball, the bowlers have to start to pitch it up and while the top-level people thought you could get him out, driving it didn't happen much at that age.'

The bread-and-butter shots for Cook in the middle of his long career breaking records at Bedford were the pull, the cut, and working the straight ball off his hip for runs. 'As he got stronger and grew,' says Farrell, 'there were certain things he was able to add – he learned to punch balls slightly short of a length back past the bowler. Really, he could play all the shots in the textbook, but nothing fancy.' Burgess notes that Cook's batting 'wasn't technically pretty on the eye but he was always very gritty.'

Cook's reputation was burgeoning across the school cricket network. In declaration matches, where a team bats until they think they have a big enough score to defend, the perceived tactic against Bedford was to win the toss, bat first, and set the opposition a ridiculous target that they could not realistically chase. 'You had to bat Bedford out of the game to stop them winning,' explains Farrell. The thing is, it didn't always work. 'Alastair could pace his innings phenomenally well. I remember one innings he played against Stowe where they left us 38 or 39 overs to get 270, and with 20 overs to go we still needed 170 to win.' It appeared a draw was inevitable, but Cook was still there and had other ideas. 'Suddenly, three overs in succession, he hit them all for 18 and he got 170 not out, won us the game with an over to spare, and that was just brilliant.'

There were other memorable games too. Against Oakham, who had Stuart Broad in the side, he hit a double century, and one renowned judge of schoolboy cricket, former Lancashire pro Frank Hayes, reckoned it was the best innings he had seen played.

Burgess remembers that Cook was also a meticulous collector of data. Keen scorers – and Bedford made a real effort to appoint a genuinely dedicated official First XI scorer each summer – often produce extra statistics and so on beyond just filling in the scores. In 1999–2003, these would have included individual 'wagon wheels' showing where all twenty-two batsmen in a match had scored their runs. 'He always had a good look at his wagon wheels,' says Burgess. 'They would be collectors' items now. He always liked to review his innings in some details after, noting down points of where he could make improvements. That's one of the reasons why he's done as well as he has done.'

Ever conscientious, Cook also appears to have had the perfect, unflappable mindset for batting. Very often, you might see a flashy, brilliantly talented batsman in a youth match hit a series of towering sixes before tossing his wicket away by taking one too many risks. Cook simply knew at this young age that he would not get carried away if he was batting well, nor would he get edgy if he was batting badly. He certainly knew that at any time he might get a really good ball, and he watched out for that.

Farrell adds on the same subject: 'We talked about the game a lot and the notes he made were probably a part of that process. Once he became captain for his last two years, we were thinking about how to get the most out of other players in the team too.'

I am keen to get Farrell to expand on Cook as a captain. There were times during his captaincy of the England team when his tactics attracted criticism. Geoffrey Boycott, during one tour of the UAE, was particularly vociferous on the issue. In 2014, Derek Pringle, writing in the *Daily Telegraph*, suggested Cook was probably a cautious captain since his school career, noting the high number of matches involving Bedford that ended up as draws. (In truth, as has been explained above, many of the draws were the products of overly cautious tactics by opposing captains, rather than Cook, and Bedford won pretty much every game that wasn't a draw.)

Farrell is unsurprisingly defensive about Cook's captaincy skills, without pouring lavish praise on this particular aspect of his make-up. 'There was a lot of onus on him to get runs, and I thought he did a really good job. It was always a bit cat-and-mouse. There's not much room for huge innovation as a schoolboy. Authenticity is a really important word for him, and that's what you got from Alastair as a captain. He wasn't completely negative. He wanted to win every game. We'd have conversations, trying to work out where a batsman's strengths and weaknesses were and the simple things – rotating your bowlers and making sure you have the right ones at the end.'

Aside from the single year in which he kept wicket, Cook also had to do his bit in the field, and, it so happens, with the ball.

Farrell says: 'By the end he'd turned himself into quite a good schoolboy off-spinner. That's what happens when you are that talented! He would bowl, he had twelve overs or so in an innings and do it perfectly reasonably. In the first-team games he would bowl quite often.

'He had to work at his fielding but he did work at it. He found his niche in the slips and worked very hard at it. He worked hard at his throwing too and developed a reasonable arm – as a young man he could throw the ball a long way and those were the days they were all working on those baseball-style throws.'

Somehow, not everyone appreciated Cook. Farrell remembers a scout from Nottinghamshire turning up to a game at Tonbridge in what was probably Cook's second or third year. 'He watched Alastair for twenty minutes and then walked off saying "he's too small". That amazed me. He didn't seem to understand that people develop at different times.'

Whatever the right thing was, Cook tended to do it. Farrell recalls an instance when, in his last year at school, he was leading the England Under-18 (or possibly Under-19) side at Canterbury in a three- or four-day game, but the last day was rained off.

'He made the effort to come back for our fielding practice on a Friday night ahead of our Saturday game. He could have done anything, gone out for a beer with some of his England mates maybe, but he made sure he was back in time to be captain for the fielding practice and nobody had told him to do that. In fact, nobody really knew if the game at Canterbury had been rained off or not but he knew what the right thing to do was in his mind. He was very genuine and very authentic.'

Physically, Cook developed much later than the average teenage boy. Photographs of Bedford games show him significantly smaller than his teammates for the first three years. Finally, he had a growth spurt before his last two summers, but he did not finish growing until after he left school. 'Some of those guys who score all those runs as a schoolboy have got all the physical advantages; Alastair scored them for other reasons – and then the physique came afterwards.'

By no means a natural athlete, Cook had to find ways to keep fit. He volunteered to join pre-breakfast morning swimming sessions – 'At first we thought he was going to drown,' says Farrell – intended more for the rugby squad to improve upper-body strength and cardiovascular fitness. If he wasn't swimming, he might be working on his fielding instead, also before breakfast, waking up his friends still tucked up in bed by noisily doing a bit of solo fielding practice just outside the dormitory windows, perhaps throwing a ball at a single stump. If Cook was going to make it, he had to work a little harder on his fitness than others – and he did. Even now, he runs for the Leighton Buzzard cross-country team. He has made himself into a natural athlete, and was England's top performer in the yo-yo endurance test, even though he was by some distance the oldest.

Cook was unfazed by academic commitments. The exam system, with its focus on the summer term, has always put pressure on cricketers and that has just got worse over the years. In particular, when GCSE year comes, a lot of talented players give up cricket for the year, and it's difficult for them to be coaxed back into the fold again. Cook continued to score runs, year in, year out, at school. On some of those long Saturday afternoons, when word got round that he was about to break yet another record, the pavilion would fill up steadily with spectators.

In 2001, when Cook was sixteen, a tour of the Caribbean was

arranged. Bedford entered a tournament in Barbados with sixteen teams, along with some other English schools and a lot of good West Indian youth sides too. Having reached the semi-finals in 1998, hopes were relatively high, especially with the team feeling they could bank on Cook's runs. 'It was a high-quality tournament and though Alastair did really well we came something like thirteenth out of the twenty sides. You get 240 in 40 overs and lose quite comfortably. We were playing on good club grounds and they varied in quality.'

Farrell has remained close to Cook and keeps in regular text-message contact with him. He travelled to Melbourne at Christmas 2017 to see him play in the Ashes Test at the MCG, reckoning it would probably be his last chance to see his protégé represent his country in Australia, so what better reason to head there for a holiday?

Australia batted on the first day, the only day Farrell and his daughter had tickets for. But Cook discovered his old teacher was in town and arranged tickets for the third day. Cook began the day on 104 and ended it on 244. England had already lost the series by being beaten in the first three Tests but this little show of defiance, of which Cook was the architect, stopped the rot and Farrell was there to see it. He also caught up with him in Sydney just before the final Test.

I ask him what it must be like sitting in that vast amphitheatre at the MCG, watching the boy he had nurtured for five years effortlessly take runs off Australia's best bowlers for ten and a half hours.

'It was lovely to see a really decent bloke signing off in Australia in a really substantial way, completing the set of scoring a hundred at all five grounds in Australia and getting the recognition from the Australian players.

'There was a great sense of pride to be associated with it but I was also just pleased for a really decent bloke to get his rewards for not changing, not allowing the trappings to get to him while not forgetting all the things that had happened along the way.

'All I did was to try and look after him and actually there came a point when he didn't need looking after any more. He had the ability to put things in perspective and to try and make sure things were done properly. In fact, he was the epitome of that.'

The students and teachers at Bedford School still see Cook from time to time. He tends to watch the First XV play a home game once a season with the same bunch of friends he grew close to in his first year at the school. They were also invited, along with Farrell, to a VIP corporate box arranged by the England and Wales Cricket Board for his final Test at the Oval.

More often than not, he turns up for the regular fixture in which the Bedfordshire Farmers take on the Masters.

The team is captained by Tom Turner, still a close friend of his, who lives up the road from him. But no special dispensation is made for Cook's commitments. 'They wouldn't change their fixture list to work round him,' laughs Farrell. 'It's a case of "this is our fixture list – let us know if you're available".' Burgess says: 'He'll come in, bat number eleven, allow one of the PE staff to get him out and then go out for a curry and beers afterwards with everyone.'

Burgess had a good view of Alastair Cook in the round, not merely from a cricketing perspective. Encouraging him to play a wide range of sports for as long as possible was a key part of his input.

'He loved the school, enjoyed all sports and played rugby right through to the end of his third year. He would play scrum-half or fly-half and obviously was fairly talented with the ball. He was also a very good squash player and he got into our first team for squash.

'Cricketers tend to have the ability to transfer their talent to other sports. His big thing, alongside his cricket, was his squash once he got to the sixth form. I don't know if he still plays now, but I'd like to think he does.'

As for his rugby, Cook was somewhat nonplussed that he never advanced further than the Colts B team in the three years he played for the school. Farrell points out: 'He's still bitter about it; he complains to me that he hasn't forgiven me that I never picked him as scrum-half for the Under-16 first team. A guy he opened the batting with, Will Notley, kept him out of the side. He's still bitter about it!'

So as well as excelling at cricket, and to some extent squash, Cook was a more-than-competent ruby player. In the spring term he kept his eye in with hockey. Burgess says: 'The boys in our first year do what they are asked to do initially. We want to keep their experience as wide as possible for as long as possible.' The decision for Cook to drop rugby for his last two years would have been made in consultation with Essex, who continued to keep very close tabs on Cook. In fact, he was now turning out for the Second XI in the holidays.

Burgess adds: 'We've got a boy in school now called Gus Miller, who's potentially a very talented cricketer, who has decided of his own accord that he wants to carry on with rugby. Playing multiple sports has got to help with spatial awareness and hand-eye coordination and some sports are a bit one-dimensional, so playing multiple sports would be beneficial for physical development too. Cooky would have done all sports up to his GCSEs and then performed well in the squash team for his last two years.'

The main room in the pavilion that allows access to the balcony is now called the Alastair Cook room. It was refurbished in 2013 and opened by Cook himself. There are portraits of some of his England exploits. There's a bat commemorating the 2010–11 Ashes, a series in which Cook scored an astonishing 766 runs, signed by the players from both teams.

A relatively small school, and with significantly smaller grounds than the likes of Eton, Harrow and Radley, Bedford has an extraordinary strike rate in terms of producing top-class sportsmen. Cook overlapped with Will Smith, a county stalwart still plying his trade at Durham. He was also in the same team as James Steadman, who played hockey for England, and Dave Callum, who played rugby for Scotland. More recently, Alex Wakely, the Northants captain, has come out of the Bedford system. And there's James Kettleborough, who broke one of Cook's batting records, before going on to play a season at Northants and two at Glamorgan. All these names appear on the little wooden boards in the Alastair Cook room, alongside two England rugby internationals, Martin Bayfield and Andy Gomarsall.

Apart from this room, the school does not overplay its association with Cook. The most recent edition of the Old Bedfordians Club magazine does not mention him. Yet there is a strong sense that his legacy will go further than the bright, airy room in the pavilion that carries his name. Indeed, the front cover of the 2018 school magazine charting the exploits of current pupils has a boy studiously leaning forward to play a forward defensive block. There is something in the angular thrust of his shoulders and knees that immediately brings to mind a right-handed version of Cook himself.

Burgess believes the evidence is fairly clear that Cook's achievements, and other attributes, have aided Bedford's recruitment drive. 'It's probably because he's conducted himself so well in the public eye, incredibly well really – it can't do anything but good for the reputation of the school. Nobody has a bad word to say about him.

'There's no doubt he's had a huge impact on cricket at the school and only in a positive way. There are a lot of boys who would come to the school purely on the basis of cricket and on the basis of what Cook did. Last summer our teams made all three national finals, the Under-15s, the Under-17s and the First XI.'

On the back of that, four players still at the school have been signed to county academies. It perhaps will not be very long before the next Old Bedfordian wins an England cap.

CHAPTER THREE

BREAKING THROUGH

After leaving Bedford in the summer of 2003, Alastair Cook had developed a reputation as a schoolboy cricketer of some note. He had not yet, however, proved he could transfer those skills to the professional environment.

With a few appearances for the Essex Second XI under his belt, he was to make his first-class debut at the end of the same summer in which he left school. Not yet nineteen, he was given his chance at the back end of a disappointing summer for Essex in which relegation from the top tier of the County Championship was already inevitable.

Ronnie Irani, the colourful Essex captain of that era, who was good enough to play in 31 one-day internationals (ODIs) and three Tests for England, liked what he saw in Cook from the word go.

'We actually first played against him when he turned out for the Essex Board XI – he was this young guy who kept wicket and opened the batting. I really strongly remember that innings from Cooky. We had guys who would bowl in our regular one-day side and had learned to bowl wicket to wicket consistently. This might have just been a friendly game, but it was competitive. Our bowlers kept on bowling to him on middle stump and he kept hitting them off his pads wide of mid-on. He scored so many runs as a young man playing that exact shot and just looking like a very mature player, solid without being a firecracker. He had no real airs and graces but had a spectacular ability and talent, and just made the game look very easy.

'Did I think he would go on and do unbelievable stuff for Essex and England afterwards? I didn't know until I started batting with him when he was starting out as a professional. He looked so organised. When I was batting with him, or when Andy Flower, with his wealth of international experience, was at the crease with him, he had this presence which showed he could fit in at the crease, and this presence that seemed to be saying to the bowler, "I will grind you down in this game before you grind me down."

'As a captain, and then as a coach, my job has been to identify talent. I used to go attitude-spotting rather than talent-spotting. Talent-spotting is an easy job – but when you identify potential success you don't identify talent. He just had the right attitude to step up as a young man straight away. It wasn't even a consideration. I've always believed in the mantra "If you're good enough you're old enough." If they've not got the talent to start with you can give them the tools to change. Everyone in the world is capable of success through having the right attitude. Not everyone has got the skills certain people are blessed with but with the right attitude you can bridge the gap.

'At the time Cooky was coming through at Essex, 2003 and 2004, we had some great people at the club who could identify both talent and attitude. There was Graham Gooch of course, Keith Fletcher still doing his bit, Darren Gough as a senior pro.'

Cook acquitted himself well in that opening game for the senior team in 2003, played in fine early September weather on a typical end-of-season dry wicket at Chelmsford. Appearing in a batting side studded with past and present Essex stalwarts – like Irani, Flower, Mark Pettini, and James Foster – Cook rebounded from a modest thirteen in the first innings to hit an unbeaten sixty-nine in the second innings. Essex won the match by nine wickets with a day to spare. Retaining his place in the final two games of the season, he hit two more fifties and ended up with the second-best average for the season in the Essex ranks, behind only Nasser Hussain who was usually absent with England commitments.

Having completed his growth spurt, Cook doubled up on his fitness regime – there was more swimming, more running, and he found he had extra scoring options. Out went the sweep, never a great option for a tall batsman, and in came the lofted drive.

Somewhat in awe of playing alongside the hugely experienced Flower and Irani, Cook was nevertheless warmly welcomed into the Essex dressing room where Graham Gooch – who would prove to be such an influence on Cook's adult career – was the coach and something of a living legend in the game, having scored an England record 8,900 runs in Tests.

In the second of those three games, a defeat to Warwickshire which sealed Essex's relegation, he faced Waqar Younis, a bona fide superstar among fast bowlers, albeit now in the autumn of his career. With typical modesty, Cook says in his autobiography, *Starting Out*, that during his second-innings fifty-five against Warwickshire, Waqar was 'not bowling particularly quickly'. He insists that once he was back in the pavilion, dismissed by a part-time spinner, that the great Pakistani began to 'crank up the pace and bowl as he did in his prime' leaving the eighteen-year-old Cook a 'spellbound onlooker'.

As autumn moved into winter, Cook now embarked on his first proper intensive spell of coaching with Gooch. It was a curious liaison on the face of it. Cook describes Gooch as his boyhood hero, which is interesting because Cook was only ten when Gooch played international cricket for the final time aged forty-one in 1995, and only nine when he hit his last Test century. Cook clearly must have watched a lot of cricket when he was very young. One of his first memories of all, aged five, is watching the Lord's Test of 1990 against India when Gooch scored his famous 333. England's best batsmen of the post-Gooch era –

Graham Thorpe, Mike Atherton, Alec Stewart – did not resonate as strongly as Gooch did with Cook. Was it the Essex connection? Or the fact that he identified with a personality trait in Gooch, a man constantly working hard at his game, the fitness addict, the doggedly determined opener?

For two months, Gooch just kept throwing balls to Cook, working on one type of shot after another. It was classic drill training, with no surprises. You work on one shot for about an hour at a time – let's say the off-drive – until you can't perfect it any further, until you know it as well as the five times table, and then you move on to the on-drive, and so on. It can't have been thrilling for either party but in terms of establishing the foundation of the player who would blossom on the international stage a few years later, this was probably some of the most crucial preparation time Cook ever spent.

In January, England announced the Under-19 World Cup squad. In terms of junior global cricket, the Under-19 World Cup is a pretty big deal. It is a televised tournament that is generally considered to be a sort of shop window of precocious talent. Usually, several players from the major sides go on to have fairly substantial senior careers. The 2004 tournament would be held in Bangladesh.

Cook was appointed as the England captain and, working on the cricket desk at the BBC Sport website at the time, I called him for a quick chat. It must have been one of his first telephone interviews but he sounded like he'd done a thousand. It was almost as though he knew he'd have to spend half his life dealing with media demands. He didn't say anything particularly memorable, and kept his answers succinct. Yet he seemed remarkably mature and composed for someone about to embark on a fairly major assignment.

England began with predictably easy wins against Nepal and Uganda, Cook opening the batting with his Essex teammate, Ravi Bopara. In the next phase, Cook scored centuries against New Zealand and Zimbabwe, and England maintained their 100 per cent record with a narrow win over Pakistan (Cook eighty-seven).

Everything had been going so well, but it came to a juddering halt in the final when England failed to chase down a target of 250 against West Indies, who marched to victory on the back of stand-out performances from Ravi Rampaul and Denesh Ramdin, familiar names to cricket followers.

Having acquitted himself exceptionally well on a personal level out in Bangladesh, Cook signed professional terms with Essex. He was happily living in the family home in Wickham Bishops again and ready to hit the ground running. Essex would be playing their Championship cricket in Division Two so, in theory, he would be facing bowlers down a notch on those against whom he had hit three half-centuries the previous summer. In theory, everything looked set fair for a big summer from Alastair Cook. But like a new band trying to produce the fabled difficult second album, Cook, for the first time in his career really, struggled. He wasn't used to anything except constant success. It must have been an alien concept.

The records show he averaged just 29.89 in first-class cricket for Essex in 2004. It was not exactly disastrous; he had a better run than Bopara, and he played in all the County Championship matches that he was available for. All the hard work with Gooch had failed to provide instant rewards. He was getting out lbw a lot and bowlers were also successfully targeting his off stump, preying on a weakness that cropped up from time to time throughout his career.

He did at least celebrate his maiden first-class century, albeit on a road of a wicket at Chelmsford and against a far-from-frightening Leicestershire attack. Essex, of course, could have chosen to drop Cook when he was unable to back up that century, scored in May, with further scores of note, but kept the faith. Impressively, they were probably taking a long-term view.

Irani remembers this phase in Cook's career well. 'Cooky didn't do too well in his first full season for us, but with somebody like that – with everything he brought to the table – you could make them or break them depending on whether you continued to show loyalty to them or not.

'As club captain at the time, I never discussed his form with him. He might have spoken to Graham about it. Could we have dropped him? Yes, but one or two players had already been around the club a long time and had had their chances. As far as I was concerned we were going to stick with Alastair.

'He struggled to get in our one-day side consistently, even though I actually think he's a good one-day player. I opened the batting with him in a couple of one-day games, and people asked: "Are you kidding Ronnie?" When I batted with him I was trying to smack it into the old hospital at Chelmsford whereas he … I knew he was either going to get a single or a four. I absolutely knew there wouldn't be a dot ball. He never missed a ball. It took him a bit of time to get into the one-day side but I made sure in the back of my mind that he held his position in the four-day side. Initially, I tried to make a case for him to get into the one-day side earlier but it was very difficult because we had won trophies as a one-day side. Later, on Twenty20 Cup finals day when he was with England, he came into the team – it was very important for him to have the experience – and we sacrificed Flower for him. It was the right decision for Andy, Essex and England.'

This was around the time English counties were beginning to fill up their squads with players on so-called Kolpak contracts. South Africans, in particular, were able to be employed under deals that meant they were treated as EU citizens and thus did not count towards the strict overseas player quota. The England and Wales Cricket Board grew to loathe this situation. They wanted counties to produce talented home-grown youngsters who could one day be in the mix for senior international recognition. The last thing they wanted was to see the counties filled up with South Africans who were past their prime and had grown disenchanted with domestic opportunities. They were competent pros; plenty had experience of top-level international cricket. However, they were essentially mercenaries.

Essex did occasionally select the odd Kolpak player, but unlike counties such as Northants and Leicestershire they were reluctant to go too heavily down that route. They can be commended for trying to bring on young players as much as possible, players like Cook and Bopara. Eventually the ECB realised they could not legally prevent teams from fielding Kolpakkers. They could, however, offer financial incentives to counties who had England-qualified youngsters. The situation is now largely under control.

Whatever Essex's reasoning, Cook has previously revealed how grateful he was to Gooch and Irani for believing in him during that 2004 summer, for giving him the miles on the clock he needed as a talented batsman and the level of competition his game merited.

While his admiration for Gooch had been established for some time, Cook was also fulsome in his praise of Irani, noting how the former England all-rounder had been able to turn himself into a specialist batsman of high class after his wonky knee had finally precluded him from bowling his brand of brisk and accurate fast-medium stuff that was often so effective in that era, particularly in limited-overs cricket.

In truth, it was remarkable how many senior players and high achievers were around the Essex set-up at that time. We have barely mentioned Flower and Hussain up to now, but they were incredibly useful pros for a young aspiring batsman to lean on for support.

Flower, in his pomp at the start of the millennium, could justifiably be regarded as one of the best players in the world, all the more remarkable since he was playing for the perennial weakling nation, Zimbabwe, and usually had to spend most of his longer innings watching wickets tumble at the other end.

The International Cricket Council (ICC) has a list which is hardly ever referred to but shows the highest all-time ranking of individual batsmen, and places Flower thirty-fifth on the list, just two below Sachin Tendulkar and one below Wally Hammond. Steve Waugh and Rahul Dravid are beneath him.

Hussain, a bristling tough nut, and former England captain who had led a striking renaissance in England cricketing fortunes from 2000 to 2003, retired from the Test team in May of that 2004 season. Unlike Cook, he did not choose to remain as a player at Essex but went straight into the Sky Sports commentary box instead.

Irani, Hussain (albeit in just two appearances), the tall opener Will Jefferson, and the veteran John Stephenson all averaged in excess of fifty in first-class cricket for Essex in 2004. Six others all averaged between thirty and fifty, putting into perspective how much Cook, a conscientious collector and recorder of statistics, must have been privately disappointed with his personal return.

Hussain had the distinction of scoring a century in both his final Essex appearance and his final Test innings that summer. Cook shared the first of those two experiences with him, contributing fifty-one, and explaining afterwards: 'That was pretty special. You cannot measure how valuable it is for a youngster like me to bat with such players as Hussain, Flower and Irani.'

The winter of 2004–05, in which Alastair Cook turned twenty, was presaged by a decision he made to once again forgo the opportunity of starting a university degree.

Almost everyone in Cook's life, from his mother, to Graham Gooch, to the second-team coach John Childs, was keen for him to return to academia. His father was non-committal about the whole thing.

Apart from anything else, Cook was already looking ahead to the summer of 2005 and the chance to put right his failures to fully establish himself in the Essex team the previous season. He wanted to give the club the return on their investment in him that they deserved. Gooch, in particular, was worried that if, for whatever reason, cricket did not work out in the long term for Cook then at least if he had a degree to fall back on a Plan B would open up more easily.

Yet nobody would convince Cook otherwise: he was determined to establish himself as a full-time cricketer and that's how it would be. Cook looked at the England top order, studded with star talent like Marcus Trescothick, Andrew Strauss, Michael Vaughan, Ian Bell and Kevin Pietersen, and mentally ruled out the possibility of chiselling his way into a Test appearance any time soon. The winter of 2004–05 and the 2005 season were all about further honing his skills, and then executing them in the heat of the County Championship.

While all his school friends to a man, even those who had enjoyed a gap year, were now at universities up and down the country, Cook checked into the England Academy at Loughborough, under the tutelage of Rod Marsh. If Hussain could be described as a hard taskmaster, then Marsh, an archetypal straight-talking Aussie who had been a high achiever in the Australian national side, was Hussain times ten.

Marsh's was a school of hard knocks, where strict hours of 9am to 5pm Monday to Thursday were maintained (presumably with some sort of break for lunch), and any slacking was clamped down on severely. Cook had no issue with that at all.

On Fridays, Cook had driving lessons, passing his test swiftly, and the weekends were roast dinners back home at Wickham Bishops. There would be a lot more packed into the winter too. Gooch, funding much of the trip out of his own pocket, arranged for him to get some outdoor cricket which, in an English winter, necessitated a long-haul flight. In Cook's case, it was to Perth, Western Australia. Former Hampshire batsman Paul Terry, best known – unfortunately for him – for having his arm broken by West Indies fast bowler Winston Davis in his second and final Test – ran an academy in Perth and after training there in the week, Cook turned out for a club side called Willerton at the weekends.

Describing his Perth sojourn as a 'mini university experience', Cook also had time to fit in a visit to another Gooch project, the Mumbai spin clinic. It was what it said on the tin: lots of batting practice, purely against local spinners, and no matches at all. Interestingly, having ruled out the sweep – one of his mainstays in his early teens – at the start of the 2004 season, Cook began practising it again. It is harder to play the shot as a tall batsman but so often a useful release shot against the slow bowlers – a good way to stop them bowling a lot of dot balls in succession. Throughout his career, Cook has continued to blow hot and cold on the sweep shot. It is a bellwether of his confidence levels if you see him bring one out early in his innings.

There was still time for Cook to shoehorn something else in during that 2004–05 off-season, as he was a late call-up to the England A squad to tour Sri Lanka. He scored one half-century in three innings, weathering seriously uncomfortable conditions of 45 degrees Celsius, with high humidity.

The proof that a fairly arduous winter – Loughborough, Perth, India, Sri Lanka – was worth the effort came at the very start of the English season in 2005. Picked for the MCC side to play champion county Warwickshire in the traditional curtain-raiser – in those days it was played at Lord's as opposed to Dubai – Cook hit 120 and 97.

As has been noted in the introduction of this book, Cook went on to enjoy a season studded with regular success. Adding those runs for the MCC to the twenty-eight first-class innings he played for Essex through the season gave him an impressive aggregate of 1,466 runs in all, at an average in excess of fifty, alongside an award as the Cricket Writers' Young Cricketer of the Year.

Many of Cook's most productive innings featured big partnerships with Andy Flower. 'It was the perfect learning experience for me and well illustrated the role of top-quality overseas players,' he wrote. 'There could be nothing better for a young left-hander than to share a stand for that length of time with another left-hander who happened to be one of the best batsmen in the world.'

From watching Flower, Cook learned how a batsman could manipulate the field by initially targeting a particular vacant area, waiting for the opposing captain to plug the gap, and then hitting to wherever the new gap was created. Flower was brilliant at that, and also played about four or five different types of sweep shots, some orthodox, some reverses. Cook would never have that level of flamboyance or diversity in his armoury, but he could certainly appreciate it and at least try to emulate it in some small way.

Despite failing to win promotion in the Championship – Essex's bowling lacked penetration in that era – Cook helped the county win the National League, a one-day tournament, with thirteen wins in sixteen matches. He signed off with a 110-ball 94 a couple of days after hitting a century against Worcestershire in the Championship. It was a run-filled season of plenty for Alastair Cook, and elevation to a higher calling was just around the corner.

CHAPTER FOUR

A HURRIED TEST DEBUT

The England cricket squad that arrived in India in February 2006 had a very different look to it than the one that had beaten Australia in that Ashes series the previous summer.

There had been a chastening defeat in Pakistan, where they were beaten 2-0 in November, relinquishing some strong positions en route to those losses. Then came the injuries.

By the time the touring party was ready to fly out to India, Ashley Giles, the first-choice spinner, was out of contention, having failed to recover from hip surgery and failed to even board the plane.

The crisis deepened once on Indian soil, and not only because of the usual stomach problems suffered by English cricketers adjusting to the local diet.

Simon Jones, a skilful quick bowler who could blend spiteful pace with wicked swing, would never play another Test, such was his unfortunate litany of injuries. On this occasion, he injured the cartilage in one of his knees and he had to be flown back.

Michael Vaughan, the inspirational captain whose positive approach had been such a key factor in England's rise as a major force in Test cricket, had tried to recover too quickly from a third knee operation. Marcus Trescothick, the stand-in captain, got as far as the second warm-up game before announcing that he needed to fly back to England for 'personal reasons' that would later be revealed to be severe depression. Vaughan and Trescothick joined Jones on flights back to England.

Suddenly, there was nobody left to open the batting with Andrew Strauss in the first Test in Nagpur. Somewhat inconveniently, the succession line of future England players, the Academy, were on a tour of their own many thousands of miles away out in the Caribbean. Inevitably, some Jules Verne-style travel plans would have to be hatched to springboard anyone from there to India, but it was the obvious place to turn to.

Alastair Cook had already been in this situation – drafted out of the Academy training camp in Loughborough the previous autumn to be added to the England squad in Pakistan when Vaughan's knee issue had flared up. Although not ultimately required in any of the Tests, Cook had the advantage of getting to know the players, the coach Duncan Fletcher, the heavily professionalised set-up with its ever-growing back-room cohort of statisticians, analysts, masseurs, media people, and more.

What was obvious was that whenever there was another opportunity to promote an opening batsman from the Academy to the senior Test side, Cook, who turned twenty-one on Christmas Day in 2005, would be the go-to kid. His double century for Essex against the touring Australians in the summer of 2005 had, in any case, pretty much ensured that.

On Valentine's Day 2006, Cook had escaped the English winter with the rest of the Academy squad to settle into the idyllic climes of Antigua. He scored a century in a warm-up match and felt confident approaching the first full 'Test' against the West Indies Academy.

But he failed to put up a meaningful score in the first innings, tickling an attempted hook off the fiery Tino Best and being caught down the leg side. Ever Mr Perceptive, Cook noticed on his return to the pavilion that Academy coach Peter Moores was no longer watching the cricket. He was instead occupied by a series of phone calls. 'It was all very odd,' recalls Cook in *Starting Out*, 'until Peter took Jimmy Anderson and me to one side and told us that we were flying to Nagpur to join the senior team on their tour of India.'

Cook and Anderson were booked on a British Airways flight departing Antigua that night. They spent a day in London, where Cook was joined by his then girlfriend and future wife Alice Hunt before taking another overnight flight to Mumbai. After a six-hour stopover, Cook and Anderson – two peas in a pod; introverted, shy even – took their final plane to Nagpur. Having barely known each other in Antigua, these two young cricketers – who would become the finest England players of their generation – were steadily breaking the ice, getting to know each other bit by bit on their marathon journey from a small island in the Caribbean to the third largest city in Maharashtra. They are now close friends who played together in 130 Tests for England.

During the single night he had spent in London, Cook had learned that he was certain to make his Test debut when reading a Teletext headline: 'Trescothick To Come Home'. There was no official word that he would replace the Somerset player, but England's only alternative was to elevate the reserve wicketkeeper, Matt Prior, and shuffle the batting order around – a most unlikely scenario.

Upon arrival in Nagpur, Cook had two nights' sleep to prepare himself for what is a momentous occasion in any professional cricketer's life. The first night he slept poorly, awoken at times by the noise of the lift, and feeling unwell after the long journey.

At breakfast, Fletcher confirmed to Cook that he would be partnering Strauss in the Test match and both were soon strapping on their pads for the final nets session, even though for Cook it was his first in India.

The England camp was in a state of shock over Trescothick's departure. 'It was up to me, an uncapped player, to attempt to fill the great man's shoes,' noted Cook in *Starting Out*.

He was invited for a game of darts by Flintoff and Steve Harmison on the eve of the match. Flintoff was now the third-choice captain, the stand-in's stand-in, and had an unusual way of dispensing wisdom, administering more hugs than words, encouraging players rather than preaching to them. His exalted status among his peers would have helped. 'If Andrew Flintoff cannot inspire you to try to emulate him nobody can,' was Cook's take on the matter.

Cook faced the second over of the match after England had won the toss and got off the mark with a pulled four off Sreesanth. Things went very well for the hastily installed makeshift opener – a return of sixty runs in the first innings. Cook was hardly in the mood for elaborate celebrations though. Familiar advice dished out by teachers, parents and coaches the world over in these situations is, 'Don't get ahead of yourself', 'Don't run before you can walk', 'Concentrate on the present'. Few disciples can have ever listened and acted on that sage advice in the way that Alastair Cook has. One half-century is only the start of the story. It is not time to relax and think to yourself that Test cricket may be a bit easier than folk have made it out to be.

Even if he had enjoyed the benefit of two years' reflection before writing about that debut England innings, Cook's summary – 'my biggest concern was getting a duck on debut, so sixty was much better than that' – was classic English anti-hubris, an almost apologetic reflection. There is little doubt that some of his great England innings could only have unfolded because of Cook's refusal to self-congratulate, to rest on any laurels, to indulge in the glow of achievement. Along with his quiet introspection and his iron will to succeed, it's a powerful character trait that has played its part in his spectacular career deeds.

England were bowled out for 393, something of a 'par' score on a typical Indian wicket. It proved enough for a seventy-run lead, and then it was time for Cook to bat again. The game was into the fourth morning by the time England batted again and now horizons had expanded somewhat. There was an opportunity to bat with more purpose this time, to set up a declaration and hope that rookie spinner Monty Panesar – who had dismissed the iconic Sachin Tendulkar in the first innings – might exploit a pitch which, it could be reasonably expected, would break up and provide assistance to the spin bowlers.

Cook, especially at this nascent stage of his career, was not someone who could bat comfortably while shifting up the gears. Nor did he completely retreat into his shell. The result was the completion of a most satisfying debut – a six-hour innings of 104 not out which was the anchor for Kevin Pietersen's much more rapid 87, allowing England to declare overnight and set India a target of 368.

Let's rewind just a little bit: this lad had just turned twenty-one. He had been ushered away in haste from the early stages of an Academy tour of the Caribbean to shore up a crisis-hit batting unit. He had just two days to acclimatise in India, the first of which was a write-off after he was hit by sickness on arrival. He had one day in the nets. Then bang – 60 and 104 on debut.

If not quite as productive in terms of runs as Strauss's England debut two years earlier – 112 and 83 – it was no less remarkable given the heavily foreshortened build-up that Cook had to cope with.

Cook and Strauss – both left-handers; both naturally self-confident without tilting towards arrogance; both possessed of a rare hunger for runs allied to a fierce will to succeed; both impressively unflappable and not easily distracted – would go on to accumulate 5,253 runs in partnership together. Only four pairings ever have been more prolific.

In Nagpur, they gelled instantly, with stands of fifty-six and ninety-five. On this occasion, it was Cook who stood out and he reached his century late on that fourth day with a well-placed back-foot punch through point for four. There were no nerves whatsoever. There is a close-up of him on YouTube waiting for Harbhajan Singh to bowl the ball he would despatch to the boundary and it shows a young man clearly relishing the moment. He's not *quite* licking his lips, but you get the picture.

Writing for the *Wisden Cricketers' Almanack*, Dileep Premachandran noted that: 'Cook unveiled a compact technique and tremendous temperament. He eased his way to a classy yet unhurried century, becoming the youngest Englishman to reach a Test hundred in sixty-seven years, and earning a marriage proposal – offered on a placard – from a pretty girl in the stands.'

Cook himself deflected much of the praise on to Pietersen, saying he would never have reached his personal milestone if there had been more pressure on him to lift the run rate; Pietersen batting at his natural tempo ensured that as a collective unit England made progress at a tick under three and a half runs per over.

'He can just hit balls that no one else can in places that no one else can find,' wrote Cook. 'On that momentous day in Nagpur, I couldn't have asked for anyone better than Kevin to partner. While I was playing out maidens, Kev just kept on hitting Anil Kumble for six. I was thinking "How is he doing that?" I can't hit a six. I certainly can't sweep a ball for six.'

Cook describes reaching that century, late on day four as '... the most extraordinary moment. I couldn't believe I had done it.

It still sends shivers down my spine just thinking about it. It's almost like a mirage. Did I actually do that? Did it happen to me? It's hard to think of anything that can ever top it on a cricket field.'

Back in England, Cook's parents had been singing at a concert the night before his landmark innings and had got home late. Sensibly, they recorded the cricket and watched it as live a few hours later, refusing to answer any phone calls. Even Cook himself had to wait until after they had calmly finished watching to get through on the phone. They congratulated him briefly, and then updated him with some trivial village news.

The apple does not fall far from the tree. Cook has said his parents' even-tempered approach to life helped him keep things in perspective even at a time when so much was coming so quickly to one so young.

It was just as well the young batsman had learned those attributes from his parents. While he briefly had time to reflect on the warm glow of that perfect debut – he made a point of remarking on how thrilled he was that everyone around the England set-up was genuinely thrilled for him – the second Test came around pretty quickly and with it, perhaps inevitably, his first taste of senior international failure: scores of seventeen and two.

The match was lost and Fletcher was critical of Cook's changed attitude at the crease – he felt he had been overly defensive, thinking too much, not allowing his natural game to come to the fore.

So the two teams went to the series finale in Mumbai. The Wankhede Stadium is one of cricket's premier venues. It delivers a real sense of occasion and after the relatively quiet atmosphere of Nagpur and Mohali this was a match that everyone wanted to be involved in. It was a chance for England, underdogs though they undoubtedly were, to come away with something to remember the tour by and the Barmy Army were out in force in a city that is probably the most accessible in the whole of India for tourists.

For Cook, disaster struck in the form of a dodgy pizza the night before the Mumbai Test. You may well ask why you would go to India and eat at an Italian restaurant, but in any event the timing of Cook's bout of food poisoning could not have been any worse.

He started feeling unwell almost immediately, and knew the game was up when, on the morning of the match, his condition worsened. Fletcher pulled him out of the match, handing over another Test debut, this time to Owais Shah, and Cook by now was so ill he could barely watch on TV as Strauss and Shah both scored runs in a total of four hundred.

England surprisingly cruised to a 212-run win that still resonates strongly in many collective memory banks, with four wickets for Shaun Udal in what proved to be the Hampshire veteran's final Test. Cook was, by now, at least well enough to be at the ground and join in the celebrations afterwards. Flintoff, whose captaincy would later be cruelly criticised on the following winter's disastrous Ashes tour, was hailed for his inspiring leadership.

It must have been a bittersweet experience for Cook, able now to include himself in the post-series celebrations but knowing he had not been able to contribute to the win. He had played a major part in the series through his unforgettable debut. Yet he had nothing to show from his second Test efforts, and selection uncertainty was bound to be a factor when he had been unable to reinforce his case in Mumbai.

That said, Cook's even-handed approach was ever his friend. He prepared for the 2006 season considering himself an

England player, as he was of course entitled to do so, but equally cognisant of the fact that his place in the team set-up was not a foregone conclusion if and when more senior batsmen were able to report fit again.

CHAPTER FIVE

HOME COMFORTS AND TEST CENTURIES

Alastair Cook claims to have slept for a week on his return from the India tour which elevated him from young aspiring county opener to successful Test-match batsman. When the serotonin and adrenaline drained away, fatigue set in.

It was natural for him to be preoccupied about whether his place in the England side could be guaranteed in the short term. The management were certain to keep a spot available for Marcus Trescothick, given the success the burly Somerset man had enjoyed for the senior team across both limited-overs and the Test-match game. He was somebody who could quickly get on top of opposition bowlers and it was ideal to have a player as dynamic as Trescothick at the top of the order. So Cook felt the need to continue to prove himself in the early part of the 2006 summer. A decent enough start evaporated when he turned out for England A against Sri Lanka in the week before the first Test and registered a duck.

But Bell had underperformed in India, with a top score of fifty-seven in six innings. The decision of the selectors, chaired at the time by David Graveney, was to incorporate Cook at number three and inform Bell – as politely as possible – that he needed to go back to Warwickshire and score lots of runs for his county.

Cook does not recall being nervous ahead of his home debut, in front of the big Lord's crowd. He felt instead that the selectors were confident in his ability, and he planned to use that confidence to his own advantage. Whereas sometimes in professional sport, as well as in professional life, the application of an extra layer of responsibility can make some people shrink in the spotlight, in Cook's case his psyche responded in the opposite way – he used the elevation to continue to improve, and to bloom in the full glare of his enhanced position as an England cricketer. Each new England cap was a springboard for growth, rather than some unwelcome burden.

Reporters who had access to Cook at this time predictably asked him what he felt about trying to fill an established 'problem' position at number three. It was difficult for him to provide a clear answer, but it is worth assessing this very particular role in Test-match cricket.

An opener always knows he will face the new ball and it is something he must mentally prepare for. This provides both advantages and disadvantages. On the plus side, an opener has time to build himself a long innings; he can expect the pitch to be at its freshest, and the bowlers too. He also knows he has the advantage to seize command of the match situation, to get himself 'in' before the spinners come on. The disadvantage is that the bowlers are at *their* freshest, and the new, hard shiny balls are most conducive to swing and seam movement. A number four or five can expect to assess the game from the pavilion for an hour or two before having to bat and can take time to view conditions while the batsmen above him in the order are dealing with the new ball – fours and fives are effectively the 'second wave' of a batting order.

So what about the number three? It is, in some respects, a hybrid role because you could be asked to face the second ball of the match or not appear at all until after lunch. There could be virtually no time to assess conditions or almost too much. It is probably best not to be too much of a thinker if you are going to be a good number three.

Some of the best batsmen ever have been number threes – Don Bradman, Brian Lara, Ricky Ponting, Viv Richards and Wally Hammond among them. Others who were not natural openers preferred to take one more step down the batting order. Among the most talented number fours, Sachin Tendulkar is the one that springs to mind. The phenomenal Mumbai maestro scored a world record 15,921 of which 13,492 came at number four. Whether through personal choice or that of his captains and selectors, he was never asked to fill the number three spot.

For Alastair Cook, in the spring of 2006, he had to find a way to make number three work for him, in order to keep his nascent England career on an upward curve. Inevitably, he did exactly that. Having first played at Lord's as a teenager for the MCC, the pitch with its camber down the middle that can cause problems for both bowlers and batsmen held no fears for him.

For the first time, England coach Duncan Fletcher was directly involved in Cook's cricketing education. The forward press, which Fletcher had devised as a means to nullify opposition spinners, was added to the Cook armoury. Since Sri Lanka had Muttiah Muralitharan, one of the best spinners ever, in the other team, that was important.

Cook, who was not a natural sweeper, would be a candidate for lbws and other dismissals if he simply looked to play Muralitharan chiefly off the back foot – the more traditional method in which to counter spin as, in theory, it allows the batsman to see which way the ball is turning, and how much, before coming up with a response. Because spinners generally bowl a little quicker through the air than they did in previous decades, this technique has its perils. By contrast, the forward press allows the batsman to get out of an ultra-defensive shell against spin. You don't have to use it to attack the bowling, but you are naturally closer to the pitch with a forward press and perfectly positioned to drive the ball if the bowler slightly over pitches.

Fletcher also explained the value of batting with his hands lower on the bat handle. Traditionally coached, Cook's natural stance had him wielding the bat from high on the handle. The corrected stance meant that, as a tall man, Cook began to adopt a sight crouched position against spin from that Lord's Test match, and other England players, such as Kevin Pietersen and Paul Collingwood were similar.

Cook also looked at videos of Muralitharan, who was considered Sri Lanka's biggest threat with the ball even though English conditions in the second week of May were hardly ideal for him. England batted first, and once Trescothick and Andrew Strauss had predictably seen off the new ball, on came Murali. Cook's initial sparring efforts against the brilliant spinner were ungainly, but Trescothick helped him and urged him to focus on the ball, rather than the hand. That was key. Conditions were good for batting and Cook got all the way to eighty-nine in England's only innings before attempting a cut shot off the seamer Farveez Maharoof. The ball was slightly too full for the shot and he edged it behind.

To see off several spells of Muralitharan at the first time of asking was an impressive effort by Cook. There is little reason to assume he would have done any better or worse in his customary position as opposed to his fill-in role as a number three. England established a dominant position in the match before failing to close out the victory – and among a rash of dropped catches by the home side, six were shelled by Cook himself.

Reading his observations of his early fielding efforts for England in *Starting Out*, it's clear that Cook was upset with himself. As an England newbie he had to occupy a number of different fielding positions, rather than become accustomed to one. At Essex, he tended to be posted at first slip. Later, he would be the regular first slip for England too, but not yet.

'I've always been a bit of an ugly mover but I'd never really seen my running style before, and watching myself on TV for the first time, I couldn't actually believe it was me,' he notes, seemingly embarrassed. He surmises that his 'rigid' movement – so distinct from some of the lithe movers of the time: Collingwood, South Africa's Jonty Rhodes and so on – was a legacy of having a late and sudden growth spurt as a teenager.

Interestingly, what he doesn't say is that the 'ugly mover' in him was also visible in his batting stroke play. Ironically, Bell, the player Cook had replaced in the side, is regarded as one of the most beautiful players to watch of the modern era. It sounds a strange thing to say and it doesn't mean that the Warwickshire man could have been a male model in another life. It is simply that his movements, the way he strides towards the ball, the angle of his elbows and knees, and the way everything is put together, is a joyous thing to watch. Observing Bell play a cover-drive on a pleasant English summer's day makes a spectator purr with inward appreciation. It's a feeling you don't get watching Cook, at any stage of his career. The motion is always slightly clunky, slightly deliberate, lacking the feline grace of Bell or some of the other technicians of the past such as Lara and Mark Waugh.

That is not in any way to denigrate Cook. The 'ugly mover' in the field that he himself recognises translates to a productive and effective batsman – the most productive and effective batsmen England have ever produced – but a batsman whose prolific output has for ever been marked by a slightly awkward bearing at the crease. Ask a batsman whether he would trade 20 per cent of his runs for a 20 per cent boost on his overall aesthetical impression, however, and he would not even entertain the idea. The only bankable statistic that counts is the runs. Unlike ice skating, diving, and ballroom dancing, batting is not a sport where artistic impression provides bonus points.

Cook scored twenty-three and thirty-four not out (including the winning runs) in the second Test which England won easily, but Sri Lanka bit back in the final Test of the series, at a strangely spin-conducive Trent Bridge. Scores of twenty-five and five were nothing to write home about on a personal level, but no England batsman covered themselves in glory in conditions that played into Muralitharan's hands.

In England, spectators regularly come out in their thousands for all five days of a Test, even when the opponent is not a marquee nation, like Australia or India. Cook loved the atmosphere, the noise and colour. He felt it was an honour to play in front of packed stands. The last thing he wanted was to return to the County Championship and its one-man-and-a-dog connotations.

The county game had to wait. Cook was called into the England one-day squad at a time of inconsistent plans and selection in the 50-over side. Frankly, England were a poor one-day side at this time, bereft of focus and strategy, though it was still a surprise to be swept 5-0 by Sri Lanka as a heatwave gripped the country and produced true wickets on which the tourists' powerful batting unit gleefully feasted.

Sri Lanka went home; Pakistan turned up in their stead. Cook felt the need for a big score: 'It may seem odd to have been getting a bit anxious about three-figure scores relatively soon after scoring a hundred on debut, but I was thinking "I've got to do it again. I can't let Nagpur be a one-off."'

With Andrew Flintoff injured, Strauss was elevated to the captaincy and Bell returned to the side but at number six, meaning Cook stayed at three. England batted first and Cook got what he wanted: a century at Lord's. Writing about it afterwards, however, he was not impressed with himself. 'It was one of the worst innings I have ever played.' And it is true – Pakistan were in a charitable mood that day. He was dropped on nought, given not out, caught behind on forty-three when he had hit the ball, and dropped on two further occasions in what was an undeniably scruffy century, but a century nonetheless.

After a draw there, England were probably under some pressure to get a positive result in the next match. Given the expectation that now accompanied them as an Ashes-winning team, it was a disappointment that, overall, they had lost more matches than they had won since the highs of that Oval Test the previous summer. To everyone's relief they won by a huge margin. Cook scored his third century, thus inking his name ever more indelibly into England's long-term plans.

Unlike the Lord's one, it was a magnificent specimen. On a wicket that had seen Pakistan bowled out for just 119 halfway through the first day, Cook batted without alarm and without giving a chance to be sixty-five not out at stumps.

A textbook straight drive early on day two got him going again and Pakistan's varied attack tried everything to unsettle him but failed to do so as he continued at his own pace; patient, unflappable – hallmarks that would define his career. One of his best shots came once he had reached the nineties, stroking Abdul Razzaq off the front foot through extra-cover.

It took him 208 balls to get to the century, with a calm nudge for a single. Then he opened up with a glorious square drive and a straight pull in the same over off Shahid Afridi. His final score was 127. After seven Tests, he had banked three centuries, an exemplary start to his career.

England went on to win the series 3-0, though the last Test had a curious ending to say the least, as Pakistan refused to take the field after tea on day four, with the match delicately poised, after being accused of tampering with the ball.

It would take some time for that particular saga to play out before the media, and on reflection it probably affected England's preparations as they looked ahead to a trip to Australia, a rare Ashes defence and what would be the sternest examination yet of Alastair Cook, the young Test batsman who was swiftly making a global impression.

CHAPTER SIX

THE ASHES – A RUDE AWAKENING

Alastair Cook noticed one or two things on his first tour of Australia as a senior player, and an established one, albeit one who would not turn twenty-two until the day before the third Test of five.

Principally, the crowds were a surprise – handing out relentless abuse from the moment the first gentle warm-up game began. There was no witty banter, just unpleasant verbal abuse. Then there was the media: unaccustomed to the Ashes defeat the Australians had suffered the previous year, their first in nineteen years, they dished out a series of intimidating headlines, each day picking on a different member of the England team to mock.

Cook noted at the time that the Australian media operated '… in stark contrast to our media, where criticism of the England team is quite commonplace.'

Marcus Trescothick, who had left the previous England tour on account of depression, succumbed once again to his inner demons and slipped away before the Tests began. England had not played particularly well in the pre-tour matches, while the Australian side, with one or two titans of the game preparing for one final, victorious hurrah, was flexing its muscles and scenting blood.

At the time, I was a journalist with the BBC Sport website and took away one abiding memory of that first Test in Brisbane. I happened to be walking up Vulture Street to the Gabba at the same time that the England tour bus slowly negotiated its final turn down a side road.

Very often, the windows of team buses at major sports fixtures are tinted, presumably so people can't peer in. On this day, the glass was fully transparent and the faces of the England players betrayed visible nerves. Drained of blood, exchanging nervous glances – they were not the faces of players psychologically prepared to give their best.

England captain Andrew Flintoff lost the toss, and Australia batted; Steve Harmison opened up with a comically wide wide; Flintoff fielded it at second slip. The tone was set. By the end of day two, Australia had declared on 602-9; England were three wickets down for very little, with Cook, restored to opening duties because of Trescothick's absence, back in the pavilion for eleven.

There was no way back from that. Cook fared a little better in the second innings (forty-three) but England were defeated by 277 runs and had just three days between Tests to fly to another city, Adelaide, and prepare for the next match.

As a team, England got everything right for the first two-and-a-bit days. Then it went horrifically wrong (or utterly brilliantly from an Australian perspective). Matthew Hoggard was bowling well and Australia were 65-3 in reply to England's 551-6 declared. However, present and future captains Ricky Ponting and Michael Clarke struck centuries on Adelaide's notoriously true wicket and Australia were eventually all out for 513, barely any kind of deficit.

With a day to go, England were 59-1 in their second innings, a lead of 97. Only one result seemed realistically possible, namely a draw, which would have at least restored some confidence for England heading to the last three Tests.

However, Australia bowled England out for just seventy more runs, giving themselves enough time to knock off a target of 168 in the final session. Summing it all up, Andrew Miller in the Cricinfo report called it 'a day dredged straight from the pit of English Ashes misery'.

Australia deserved a huge slide of credit too. The champion leg-spinner Shane Warne and the brilliantly incisive pace bowler

Glenn McGrath would push very hard for places in any all-time world cricket team and were both in their element that day.

What was worse for a young Cook was that he had failed to contribute in either innings. Not only that – for the first time an opposition team had successfully targeted an individual weakness. This is something that is now commonplace but had not really been fully explored in Test cricket until John Buchanan took the reins as Australia coach in 1999 and embarked on an extraordinary run of success – seventy wins in eighty-nine Tests and both World Cups he contested in his tenure. Buchanan had inherited an exceptionally good group of players and ensured he got the most out of them. With hard-nosed captains to back him up – first Steve Waugh, and then Ponting – he helped instil a highly effective win-at-all-costs culture that blew up in the Aussies' faces so spectacularly with the astonishing cheating revelations that surfaced last year.

Before any series began, Buchanan would get hold of videotape of opposition batsmen, rope in squads of consultants and listen to the advice of his captains and other senior players. He would find the Achilles heel in a particular player, and in Cook's case it was all about maintaining a strict line on off stump, eliminating the width he needed to score his runs. Buchanan needed his bowlers to keep plugging away on that very specific line to Cook. He didn't want them bowling outside off stump, because Cook was a good leaver of the ball, and he didn't want them testing out middle and off, because Cook could work that one to the leg side. Bang on off stump was where to go. Cook later acknowledged the great skill, accuracy and persistence of Australia's bowlers: 'They never gave me anything to cut or short enough to leave … I was worried about my form. It was the most testing of circumstances.'

While England, as a collective unit, failed to respond to the crisis, Cook did, in the third Test at Perth. It was the second innings and England needed a highly improbable 557 to win, a target that effectively became impossible when Andrew Strauss was trapped lbw by Brett Lee on the fourth ball of the innings.

Amid the wreckage, Cook chiselled out a typical Cook century, thus becoming the first man not yet twenty-two to score four in Test matches for England. Rod Marsh, the former Australian wicketkeeper and a highly sought-after coach, writing on the eve of Cook's first Ashes century, was by now predicting huge things for the youngster.

Marsh's piece for *The Guardian*, which appeared in online editions an hour or so before Cook set out compiling his century, noted an 'uncanny' similarity between the English player's technique and the Australian Michael Hussey, at the time producing the most powerful numbers of any batsman in world cricket.

He observed that slight weakness around off stump – the same weakness that affected a young Hussey and delayed his introduction into the Australian set-up. But he admired much about Cook too:

'Anyone who saw him get that whack on the head at short leg in Adelaide will know the kid has courage. How many players would have stayed on the field and still be prepared to get in there at that suicide position? If that wasn't proof enough of his courage, what about those two magnificent hook shots off Brett Lee, thunderbolts late on the first evening of the Perth Test match?'

Two and a half years earlier, Marsh had been contacted by Tom Moody, coach of Worcestershire, who told him he had 'never seen a better young batsman in all his time in England.'

He sought the opinion of Graham Gooch, the man who to this day probably knows more about Cook's game than anyone else, and it all added up for Marsh, whose own involvement with Cook had been limited to overseeing his development on the 2004–05 Academy tour of Dubai and Sri Lanka. (Cook barely played competitively on that tour, with more experienced players preferred).

But, by now, Marsh had formed a complete enough picture about Cook to make the following prediction: 'Cook will probably captain England before he is thirty and will probably average fifty in Test cricket. He is thirsty for knowledge and when the post-mortems are written about this Ashes series he may not rate a mention. He'll remember the series for the rest of his life, though, because he will have taken so much knowledge from the contest.'

England were swept 5-0 in Australia, a most chastening reverse in which the captaincy of Flintoff – standing in for Michael Vaughan as he had done in India – came in for some sharp criticism. He failed to gel with coach Duncan Fletcher, whose days were also numbered.

But Cook's education was continuing apace. And Marsh's prediction wasn't far off either. Cook's first Test of fifty-nine as England captain would come in 2010, a long way before his thirtieth birthday. He did not, as it happens, finish with an average in excess of fifty, but his overall record was pretty good, one way or another.

CHAPTER SEVEN

INTERNATIONAL CREDENTIALS

There is an ugly euphemism bandied about these days when people – not the people that matter, mind – think they have identified somebody who might have the mettle and nous to be captain of the national cricket team at some point in time. That person is identified as an 'FEC' – future England captain.

By making the twenty-two-year-old Alastair Cook captain of the MCC for the opening domestic fixture of the 2007 season – a four-day match at Lord's against reigning champions Sussex – the England selectors were not exactly employing any great subtlety. They reckoned Cook was the sort of person who might one day be on a small shortlist of future England captains – there, I've said it! – and here was a chance to see how he went about the job in a low-profile environment.

In fact, the England management went a step further and encouraged Cook to seek the wisdom of Mike Brearley, a man pigeon-holed as the most cerebral of thinkers in English cricket. Brearley, famously, had been the last of a very rare breed of men. His playing ability was not good enough to merit a place in an international side, but he more than made up for the shortfall of runs with captaincy skills of rare ability.

Most famously, he inspired a disenfranchised Ian Botham to draw on his outlandish ability to turn around the 1981 Ashes with a series of remarkable individual performances with bat and ball.

Despite having been given Brearley's great bible on cricket leadership, *The Art of Captaincy*, by his father at the age of fourteen, Cook hadn't actually read the book in full. He probably learned everything laid out in the book and more when spending three hours in conversation with this most cerebral of individuals.

One's thoughts go back to what his Bedford teacher Jeremy Farrell said on the subject of Cook and advice – that he was very good at listening to all these people who wanted to talk to him, but also very good at filtering out the majority of the conflicting noise. Cook could not be expected to truly distil the brains of Brearley, the gumption of Hussain, the brio of Irani, along with the thoughts of Gooch, Flower and everyone else who came to him with various strands of advice – and then alchemise it all into something meaningful. That would have been an impossible task. Ignoring the bulk of it and simplifying everything as much as possible was bound to pay more telling dividends.

It is telling as well that Cook didn't really consider the captaincy a big deal – in truth, telling Steve Harmison and Matthew Hoggard that they needed an extra man in the slips would not have been a way to curry favour with England's two most experienced fast bowlers. Cook felt the biggest thing for him at that stage was to keep scoring runs.

It's important, though, that not everyone would have been quite so passive in this scenario. Consider the case of South Africa's Graeme Smith, who was appointed captain of the national side in the wake of the team's calamitous World Cup exit on home soil. He was also twenty-two, the same age that Cook was for that MCC fixture, and was quite vocal in revealing that if some of the senior players in the side needed a kick up the backside he wouldn't be frightened to administer one.

As it happens, Cook, as he so often did, marked an important fixture with a big score, batting for five hours to hit 142 against Sussex. It seemed that every time Cook was involved in a landmark match from a personal point of view, he scored a big one: the match at Bedford against his own First XI aged fourteen, the one at Chelmsford against the Australians in 2005, his Test debut. It was a good reputation to have – to excel in the same spotlight that can shrivel less hardy souls.

Kicking off 2007 with a century at English cricket's headquarters gave Cook that little spring of confidence to take into the rest of the summer. The runs flowed for Essex – the hours he'd put in on that slight technical deficiency around off stump having paid off – and he benefited from not being involved in the World Cup squad who had performed with such indistinction in the West Indies. The tournament had ended on a bitter note, with the resignation of England's coach Duncan Fletcher.

Cook was pleased to see Peter Moores appointed in his stead. Many, privately, were less enamoured and their fears were ultimately proved right. Moores, the former Sussex wicketkeeper, excelled as a county coach and at the Academy, but he lacked the required gravitas and X factor to make a success of the biggest coaching job in English cricket.

Anyway, at that point in 2007, Cook perhaps felt Moores' softly spoken enthusiasm was the perfect antidote to the blues England were feeling after a winter in which the Ashes whitewash had been followed by a limp World Cup exit. Frankly, the one-day set-up was a shambles and it would take a long time to resurrect the team's fortunes in 50-over cricket.

Though they picked off the minnows, England were beaten by New Zealand, Sri Lanka, Australia and South Africa. That rendered their final Super Eights match against West Indies academic, as by that point they could not then reach the semi-finals. It was pretty much as horrible a tournament as they could have envisaged – even though India and Pakistan somehow failed to even make it to the last eight!

Flower entered the England set-up for the first time as batting coach, a perfect dressing-room foil for Cook although of course Essex – who had also lost Irani and Darren Gough at around the same time – were expected to feel the pinch. Cook's flatmate Mark Pettini was appointed the new Essex captain, the youngest ever at Chelmsford at just twenty-four, and it proved to be a difficult baptism for him, partially because he had not really cemented a spot in the side and the runs did not suddenly start flowing for him.

Cook felt a little helpless, but there was little he could now do to help one of his best mates in the Essex set-up because his England commitments soaked up nearly all his time. He was involved in just three of the sixteen County Championship games and Essex relied heavily on Ravi Bopara for runs that season.

For England, the new regime under Peter Moores did not quite hit the ground running. The team was held to a draw by a weak West Indies side in the opening Test at Lord's with Andrew Strauss (pointedly, not Andrew Flintoff) standing in for Michael Vaughan as captain after the latter had found a new injury to rule him out of the role. Vaughan returned for the second match in Leeds, which England won along with the next two to emerge with a 3-0 verdict against the men from the Caribbean.

Cook's contributions were an extremely pleasing 105, 65, 42, 60 and 106 from the first three Tests before he blotted his copybook slightly with 13 and 7 in tougher conditions in Durham.

As is the norm in the English summer, the focus then switched temporarily to one-day cricket. Vaughan resigned the one-day captaincy and England then announced a squad without the Yorkshireman named in it. The chief beneficiary was – surprise, surprise – Cook. The new captain, Paul Collingwood, led a new-look squad, with Strauss another to be dispensed with.

The problem was that England had replaced two good batsmen who were just a little bit too slow for one-day cricket, with two more good batsmen who were just a little bit too slow for one-day cricket. In truth, though there was the odd brief high point, the lack of imagination in England selection in one-day cricket would plague the team's fortunes for a long time hence. It was only really until after two more bad World Cups for England, those of 2011 and 2015, that caution was finally dispensed with and the team was stuffed with naturally aggressive players, and naturally aggressive players alone.

In a rebuilding phase at this point, it probably would not have come as a major concern that the first bilateral one-day series after the World Cup was lost 2-0. Nor should the selection of Cook, who had played two ODIs the previous summer, have in itself been considered a questionable appointment.

However, you look back at that team who lined up for the first ODI versus West Indies and can only query its balance in terms of batting. For a start, with Dimitri Mascarenhas coming in at seven, there was very little depth; and with Cook, Bell and Collingwood in the same team (and Andrew Flintoff injured) that left the only obvious supply of fast runs being Kevin Pietersen and Owais Shah – and Shah had not exactly set the world alight with his ODI exploits up to then.

Perhaps strangest of all was that Matt Prior, who had batted at seven in the Tests, was suddenly opening alongside Cook in the one-dayers. England won the opening ODI, despite being bowled out for 225 batting first (Cook 29 from 54 balls). They failed to chase down a target of 279 in the second ODI and in the third fell almost 100 runs short of a target of 290. Cook failed to reach twenty in both those two matches.

Even given the fact that this was a few years before scores in excess of three hundred became commonplace, it was clear that the first iteration of a new-look England one-day side had suffered a batting malfunction. There would be any number of further failed attempts to get the balance right over the next few years.

There followed a series against India, always a fixture to look forward to, and in this case the tourists would be still be smarting a little after losing that Mumbai Test a year and a bit earlier.

This was an India side with some near-legendary figures approaching the twilight of their careers. Sachin Tendulkar, Rahul Dravid and Sourav Ganguly, in contrasting styles, had frustrated some of the world's best bowlers for many a year. Anil Kumble, who bowled quick leg-breaks that tended to hurry on to the right-hander, was a highly proficient spinner. Nevertheless, in English conditions, the hosts were expected to come out on top. The script was largely followed in the opening Test, even though Harmison and Hoggard were unavailable with injuries.

James Anderson, who had far from cemented his Test spot at this stage in his career, and Ryan Sidebottom carried the attack manfully to bowl the Indians out for just 201, with England hitting 298 and 282 either side of that. It left India with a very tough target of 380.

With a lot of rain throughout the match, time was not on England's side to finish off the job and the forecast on the final day was poor. But England's bowlers kept chipping away until, with thick black clouds threatening overhead, umpire Steve Bucknor rejected an appeal from Monty Panesar against last man Sri Sreesanth that looked like it had an awful lot going for it.

This was in the era prior to the Decision Review System; not only that, umpires could offer the light to batsmen if it was getting a bit dark rather than flick on the floodlights. The Indians gleefully accepted the offer and although there was still half a day to go in theory, once it started raining it did not stop.

That set the tone for an extremely frustrating series for England. Moral victors at Lord's they may have been, but they were beaten fair and square at Trent Bridge with left-arm swing bowler Zaheer Khan bowling tremendously well. So when India got to the final at the Oval, batted first and racked up 664 on the first two days, that was effectively that.

On a personal level, Cook had done perfectly adequately even if a top score of sixty-one across his six innings was less than he would have hoped for. He couldn't score centuries every game. Frankly, six hundreds in his first seventeen matches represented a pretty phenomenal return for someone who was still in his educational years as a technician.

On that note, there was some comment in the media which Cook had picked up on, noting that he was dismissed lbw in his first four innings in the series against India. That in itself was not a huge concern; what might have been was the fact that two of those dismissals were triggered by Ganguly, a part-time medium-pace bowler who could find a modicum of gentle swing but should not have been a threat to someone of Cook's ability. The theory was that having worked so hard to tighten up his technique around off stump, Cook was prone to moving his front leg closer to the line of the ball and that could then leave a left-handed batsman exposed to the one that straightened off the wicket.

Cook retained his place in the one-day squad but he needed a score in this format – and he got one straight away, a century (102, to be precise) at the Rose Bowl. A really exciting series featuring seven matches between the two teams which, thankfully, not disturbed by the weather, went all the way to a decider at Lord's on 8 September. Cook, however, found himself dropped from the team again, which looked a perplexing decision. Even though he had registered three single-figure scores in succession, he had added important contributions of thirty-six and forty to his opening hundred. Incidentally, England opened with Prior and Luke Wright in that last match – and both scored ducks.

The international calendar rolled on, and on and on, as it tended to. Just consider that this was prior to the days of the Indian Premier League and the myriad of other Twenty20 tournaments around the world. And yet, no sooner had India departed than England were off to the inaugural Twenty20 World Cup in South Africa (without Cook, who had little experience of the format). The ECB tries to keep October as an important month off for rest and rehabilitation for players now, but there was no such luxury in 2007. Instead, there was a rather peculiar split tour of Sri Lanka – five ODIs at the start of October and then a Test tour much deeper into the winter, with the first of three Tests scheduled to start in December.

Cook was back in the starting side for the ODIs but struggled to get going in the first match in which England were chasing 270 to win. On a typical low, slow pitch in the subcontinent, it is dangerous to fall behind the required run rate, and Cook took eighty balls to compile his forty-six. Thus, when he was sixth man out shortly after the halfway point of the innings, England had reached only 102 and were never going to haul in the target even with a lower-order rally.

Cook barely contributed in the next two matches but the bowlers did the hard work as England ground out wins in games two and three. Sidebottom and Anderson were by now in their element and England's batsmen were left with 212 to win in game four. Cook, batting at a much more suitable tempo than he had in the opening match, scored a good chunk of those himself with a composed eighty in a big stand with Kevin Pietersen.

Somewhat surprisingly, England had won the series and Cook had helped them do it. Question marks over his long-term future in the one-day squad would remain, but after spending the back end of October and half of November at home, it was time for Cook and England to head back to Sri Lanka and concentrate on his forte: the five-day game. A three-match Test series awaited.

Andrew Strauss had been a slightly surprising omission from England's squad. True, his form had gradually tailed away since his instant success in his first two years for the national side. That left Cook opening the batting with Michael Vaughan, and the first Test was hugely disappointing for England, who secured a good ninety-three-run lead on first innings before losing their way alarmingly in the second half of the match to go down by eighty-eight runs. It was worse for Cook himself, who was dismissed in the first over of each of England's two innings.

What followed was pretty remarkable. Cook rebounded from a thoroughly forgettable baptism in Sri Lanka to hit 81 and 62 in the second Test at Colombo's Sinhalese Sports Club, and then 13 and 118 in the finale in Galle. So what triggered the transformation in form?

Four days spent with Andy Flower on the bowling machine is what worked the oracle. Cook might have been expected to have his work cut out by Sri Lanka's champion wrist-spinner Muttiah Muralitharan, but it was the left-arm swing and seam of Chaminda Vaas which had flummoxed him in Kandy before he'd even got as far as dealing with the variations of Murali.

The bowling machine was set up to replicate, as best it could, the precise angle of delivery that Vaas would be expected to produce – not so much the movement off the wicket or in the air. Hours upon hours of learning by rote, with Cook also concentrating on delaying his movement towards the ball as long as possible, was the key – it was hoped – to establishing himself as less of a sitting duck for Vaas to knock over. Muralitharan was, of course, the other significant obstacle to overcome, but the ethos was: let's at least get past the new ball and then see what transpires.

What transpired, firstly, was the sort of batting-friendly wicket that is often described as a 'shirtfront'. England won the toss and Vaughan, batting at a faster rate than any other batsman would in the entire match, started caressing boundaries at will. Cook, scoring at barely half Vaughan's rate, helped the captain put on 133 for the first wicket with Vaughan, and, by the time he was out, had seen off almost the whole of day one. He had got through Vaas. He had got through Muralitharan. He was finally given out lbw by an umpire who was clearly more tired than he was – the delivery from Lasith Malinga would have certainly missed leg stump.

Cook's method for dealing with Muralitharan was to listen to advice he had once gleaned from Marcus Trescothick (who wasn't in Sri Lanka): play the ball as you see it out of the hand, and then off the pitch, rather than attempt to make snap judgments based on the bowler's wrist position at the moment of delivery. By being a left-hander, Cook had an immediate advantage against Muralitharan, who has always preferred spinning the ball sharply into right-handers or deceiving them with the one that goes the other way. For whatever reasons, his variations never looked quite so spiteful against a high-quality left-hander, unless the pitch was a poor one.

The Test looked like being drawn from some way out, and with all the batsmen getting runs other than the newcomer Ravi Bopara, England went to the finale in Galle. This picturesque ground is famous for its imposing fort, built by Portuguese settlers in the sixteenth century, on one side. The ground had been devastated by the tsunami of Boxing Day 2004 before funding was secured, following a major appeal, to rebuild it. This Test had long been singled out as the perfect opportunity to present the new Galle Stadium to the world, but the fates had not yet finished with the venue. Heavy rain in the weeks preceding the match had left the pitch underwater and much of the stadium infrastructure unfinished.

Cook had visited the town just two months after the tsunami when touring with the England A squad, and he notes in *Starting Out* that he found it a 'very emotional' experience to assess how far the redevelopment had progressed. England players spent much of the period leading up to the Galle Test, which was almost switched to another venue because of the flooding, making visits to various charitable and humanitarian projects. Eventually, the rain relented enough to persuade the authorities to go ahead with the match, and England won the toss and elected to bowl. This was a pretty unusual tactic. Only 18 per cent of captains, when winning a toss in a Test in Asia, choose to allow their opponents first use of the strip.

England felt, however, that the pitch would still be damp enough to make batting awkward to begin with, before drying out from the second day. In the event, Sri Lanka accepted the invitation happily, and racked up 499-8 declared. Home skipper Mahela Jayawardene delighted the home supporters with an unbeaten 213. England were then bowled out for a stunningly woeful eighty-one featuring four wickets for Vaas and two run-outs. Unsurprisingly, they had to follow on. Sri Lanka's worst friend continued to be the weather, taking out large chunks of time and making the draw much more accessible for England. However, Vaughan's tourists only got out of jail because Cook was able to produce a rearguard masterclass, occupying six hours and twenty minutes, not including the frequent weather interruptions which required him to switch off and switch on again in the manner he came to perfect over the years. Cook's 118 came off 285 balls and featured 12 fours. But none of that really mattered. What mattered was that he found a way to deal with Vaas and Muralitharan – the latter did not dismiss him once in the course of the series.

This is one of those Cook centuries that stands the test of time at this moment when we are able to reflect on his career in the round. Writing in Cricinfo, Andrew Miller told his readers: 'Cook's bloodymindedness came bubbling to the fore as he dug in against Muttiah Muralatharan.' *The Guardian* noted that it contained 'punchy back-foot drives and typically obdurate defence' while Rob Bagchi in the *Daily Telegraph* ranked it the fifth most impressive out of all of Cook's centuries.

'None of Cook's centuries have displayed more fortitude, skill and stubbornness than his match-saving century in Galle,' wrote Bagchi. 'England would have been thrashed but for him.'

One particularly hard-to-impress group of travelling English supporters watched this latest Cook masterclass behind a banner that read: 'England: Hang Your Heads in Shame'. Or perhaps they were so gripped by Cook's riposte that they forgot it was there.

As England headed for the departure lounge to spend Christmas at home with their families, Cook could reflect on one stat that hinted at the kind of scope he had as a player, and the sheer volume of runs he could be expected to give the national side for many years hence. Not yet twenty-three, he had already reached three figures seven times in Test matches. Only Don Bradman, Javed Miandad and Sachin Tendulkar had scored so many Test hundreds at such a young age.

England, however, two-and-a-bit years on from winning that famous Ashes series and with the world seemingly at their feet, were losing their way a little. Some tough decisions were needed from the selectors. Matt Prior, after making too many basic wicketkeeping errors, and Cook's Essex teammate Ravi Bopara, who had really struggled in Sri Lanka, were both dropped for the tour to New Zealand in early 2008.

Andrew Strauss was back in favour, however, and would slot in at number three in the Test side, with Cook and Vaughan booked to continue their opening partnership. As it transpired, Cook would remain at the top of the order for the remainder of his England Test career.

CHAPTER EIGHT

TURMOIL AT THE TOP

The one-day series came first in New Zealand, and proved something of a write-off for the tourists. England lost it 3-1 (with one match tied), generally not adapting as well as their typically resourceful hosts to some tricky batting conditions, with a lot of awkward wickets, rain, Duckworth–Lewis adjusted targets and so on.

Cook emerged as the heaviest run-scorer of the series, but it should be stated at this point that in all the opportunities he had in one-day cricket for England, he never quite got hold of the bowling in the sort of dominant manner required for the format. In this era, batsmen were not quite as explosive as they are today, but they were generally aggressive once the platform was set.

England, who had pretty much sleepwalked through the 2007 World Cup, continued to find it harder to drop the shackles as easily as other teams, and Cook was, arguably, part of the problem. Consider the fourth match of that series in New Zealand. England batted first and on a flat wicket at Napier (quite unlike most of the others in the series) totalled 340-6. It sounds a good score, but Cook took eighty-eight balls for his sixty-nine runs, whereas everyone else was scoring at well over a run a ball. Even Paul Collingwood, not the biggest hitter by any means, blasted an unbeaten fifty-four off thirty balls. In the end, England only tied the game, and surely it would have occurred to Cook that if he had been a tiny bit bolder in his innings they would have won it.

Perhaps this is harsh criticism, but while any appraisal of Cook as a cricketer is going to largely paint an extremely positive portrayal of a superbly accomplished and driven Test player, it would be wrong to ignore the fact that he did not quite have the required gear-shift to be an unbridled success in the one-day game. Success in full one-day internationals is about finding ways to hit the good balls for four and six. Cook could score quickly in county cricket and often also scored rapidly in warm-up matches on England tours. In both those scenarios, he received a higher percentage of bad balls to put away. But he never quite hit the high notes in ODIs themselves.

After the New Zealand series, England reconsidered their priorities and Cook played only two more ODIs in 2008, none whatsoever in 2009, and only three in 2010. After another World Cup failure (in India in 2011), there was yet another reassessment and Cook re-emerged in England's plans, not only as a regular player but as the captain all the way through to the end of 2014.

Finally, the plug was pulled altogether on Alastair Cook's career as a one-day player, following ninety-two innings yielding five centuries and an overall strike rate of a tick above seventy-seven runs per hundred balls. He played just four Twenty20 internationals.

Back to 2008 and the Test series in New Zealand, which started badly, with a defeat in Hamilton. Crisis time. England had failed to win seven Tests in succession and were on their way to three series defeats in a row in the long format. There were more changes. Matthew Hoggard (who would never play for England again) and Steve Harmison were both left out amid a feeling that the wheels of change were turning fairly quickly.

England, to their credit, recovered well to win the series. Cook provided his fair share of runs – forty-four and sixty in the second Test in Wellington – while there was an important century from the new wicketkeeper Tim Ambrose which helped England establish an early advantage.

The new-look bowling attack – featuring Stuart Broad and James Anderson for the first time in a Test together, alongside the on-form Ryan Sidebottom – knitted together well and the eventual margin of victory was a comfortable one: 126 runs.

Incidentally, that was the first of 111 matches featuring Cook, Broad and Anderson together. They would prove to be critical in England's rise to global Test match ascendancy in the subsequent years and a mainstay in the rollercoaster period that followed. If all three were fit, they nearly always played, with the occasional exception of one or two matches on wickets in the subcontinent which required enhanced spin options.

In the decider at Napier, Vaughan's decision to bat first looked highly dubious when England lost their first four wickets for thirty-six, but a fine century from Kevin Pietersen allowed the tourists to pick themselves up from the canvas and Sidebottom was then irresistible as England once again established a healthy first-innings lead. They ultimately won by 121 runs after a huge score of 177 from Strauss in the second innings.

One of the features of Alastair Cook's long tenure in the England camp has been that there has not been a lot of consistency when it comes to the identity of his opening partners. On debut he was teamed up with Strauss, and after his brief demotion to number three to accommodate Marcus Trescothick, he was back opening with Strauss for three straight series before Vaughan became his partner during the 2007–08 winter.

At the start of the 2008 season, however, things changed once again because Vaughan announced he wanted to drop down to three to help him concentrate on his captaincy. Cook had quite enjoyed working with Vaughan at the top of the order, because having a right-hander at the other end who tended to score his runs through the off-side contrasted so markedly to his own style, a left-hander working straight balls to the on-side.

The perceived thinking was that a Cook-Strauss combination – ostensibly because they were both left-handers but also because they were not that stylistically different – would make it easier for opposition bowlers to find a groove with the new ball. But the truth is Cook and Strauss had already featured in a century stand together for the second wicket – against Pakistan at the Oval in 2006 – and they hit the ground running as a combo when they renewed their liaison as openers in the first Test of the 2008 summer and immediately both scored fifties in a 40-over partnership worth 121. In the sort of unimaginative bit of scheduling that seems to be commonplace, New Zealand were once again the opponents.

For Cook, it proved to be a strange summer in which he got plenty of starts but failed to go on and make a major score. Against New Zealand he went 61, 19, 28, 6 and when they departed and were replaced by a more potent South African team there was a slightly better run of scores from Cook's bat, but there remained a frustrating lack of fulfilment – 60, 18, 60, 76, 9, 39, 67.

Cook described the season in candid terms in *Starting Out*. 'The 2008 season started to unravel for me. I just didn't feel 100 per cent right. It was hardly a crisis because the half-centuries were still coming, but I will never be totally satisfied with my own form unless I'm scoring hundreds, and the 2008 season became a matter of me working on my balance at the crease.'

It must be a source of immense frustration for high-class professional sportsmen when they enter a period of below-par performance. All those years of hard work, listening to advice, working your way up the age-group levels, into regional, national and international competition, coming somewhere close to peak form – and then, suddenly and for whatever reason, something just isn't quite right any more and you have to refocus. Don't panic. Don't think too much. Just try to get back to where you were.

It says a lot for his tenacity that he was able to graft his way to a number of sixty-odd scores in Test matches though he was aware that something was wrong with the inner mechanics in his game.

Others have been less fortunate when the form starts to mysteriously evaporate. Monty Panesar, who at the time of publication remains an active cricketer of thirty-seven, went on Twitter appealing for club sides to give him a season. He included his agent's phone number in the request.

It has been quite a ride for the eccentric Monty, who played his last Test in 2013 (and, in truth, was something of a fringe player for England from the Ashes series of 2009 onwards). It even got to the point where he was not playing well enough to get into county sides.

The reason all this is relevant is because in the second Test against New Zealand at Old Trafford in 2008, Panesar produced an outstanding spell which turned a game sharply favouring the Black Caps back in the balance, and England went on to win a match in which they had trailed by 179 runs on first innings.

Cook and Panesar got on well, delighting in each other's successes. Cook was moved to write of Panesar's performance in Manchester: 'Monty was brilliant. He really is a match-winner when conditions suit him. I think he has the potential to be England's best-ever spinner.'

Perhaps equally gifted in his own domain as Cook was in his, Panesar was someone who was unable to reboot when the going got tough and the good times came less frequently. Cook, as we will explore, was tremendously good at doing whatever he needed to do to dig himself out of a crisis, frequently pulling out the huge score he needed to quash any suggestion he might require a rest from Test duty. One of the most phenomenal statistics of all is that apart from the untimely sick bug that stopped him appearing in what would have been his third Test in 2006, he didn't miss a single game. His 159 consecutive appearances constitute a world record, and only four other players have managed more than a hundred.

Importantly, England won the home series against New Zealand 2-0 for an overall home-and-away aggregate scoreline of 4-1 against those opponents. South Africa would prove a tougher nut to crack, however. And there was to be plenty of drama on the horizon.

Around that period, the Lord's wicket had a tendency to flatten out during the course of a match and that set up a really frustrating draw for England in the series opener against South Africa. The hosts had played beautifully for three days but then had to strive for wickets across the last two days, and Sidebottom and Anderson went down with injuries as a weakened side lost the second match at Headingley. There was now major scrutiny surrounding Vaughan, part of it pertaining to the strange selection of Darren Pattinson for that match. Vaughan had gambled on the virtually unknown Pattinson because of his ability to bowl a full length and obtain swing. Chris Tremlett, who had much clearer credentials, was omitted.

Writing in the *Daily Telegraph*, Simon Briggs pulled no punches, feeling Vaughan's game was in decline: 'He has entered another form rut in which his footwork has become hesitant and his decision-making around off stump has been exposed by Dale Steyn's skiddy swing. It is a grim outlook for Vaughan, who admitted last night that England had been destabilised by the two changes made on the morning of the match. He faces his sternest test since he returned from his knee injury to score a fairytale century fourteen months ago.'

Although my own anecdotal evidence suggests they have softened their tone in the last three or four years, English cricket journalists have pretty strong opinions which bubble to the surface frequently. They have a way of turning what, at the outset, looks to the reader to be a standard news report into a bristling opinion-editorial.

For the time being, Cook was considered immune to this. Not part of the leadership team in England and generally more secure in his role than the majority of his teammates, there was no harsh scrutiny on what he was doing. In time, this would most certainly change. For now, the individual in the crosshairs for writers like Briggs was Vaughan.

The reaction from the captain was not quite instantaneous. It took a further defeat, in the third Test at Edgbaston, to persuade Vaughan that now was the time to stand down, which he did, tearfully, at a news conference where it was impossible not to feel great sympathy for the man. Vaughan had been inspirational in leading England to that extraordinary and historically significant 2005 Ashes; he had come extremely close to lifting a rare major trophy in one-day cricket when England hosted the 2004 Champions Trophy, and his batting in 2002 was spectacular, when he hit a remarkable 1,481 Test runs in the year.

He had also worked so hard through some pretty debilitating injuries, but sentiment had changed and was no longer in his favour. Vaughan's departure was a significant moment, and though Strauss had already captained England five times, winning three times and drawing the other two – and in some ways appeared the perfect man to pick up the baton – instead

Pietersen was given the job. This was because Collingwood had also relinquished the one-day captaincy and England wanted a man to do both jobs.

Here, though, is the surprising thing about that transferral of power. Cook wrote: 'When the news broke, I must admit it did cross my mind that I might be a candidate to succeed him [Vaughan] ... I did wonder whether this might be my time.' One thinks back to his schooldays, the presumption that he should be playing alongside eighteen-year-olds as a diminutive boy of fourteen. That little touch of arrogance, of sniffing out any opportunity to move up the ladder, probably lends itself extremely well to batting for long, long periods of time. A steely determination to make the most of himself was clearly allied to his grim refusal to yield to the most skilful and intelligent bowlers.

The terrorist attack on the Taj Mahal Hotel in Mumbai came at a time when England were engaged in India, though some distance away from the scene of the horror. Cook remembers being on a late-night bus ride from Cuttack, where England had lost the fifth one-day international, to the team's hotel in Bhubaneswar when the news started trickling through that something terrible had happened.

Cook was one of a number of players who were keen to get out of India as soon as possible, with the Tests yet to be played. 'It seemed a very volatile situation to us,' he wrote. 'There had been reports that, in Mumbai, Westerners had been targeted by the terrorists. Should we be carrying on playing cricket in those circumstances?'

Certainly, if there was an escalation in violence and the incident in Mumbai was the start of a concerted campaign by a terrorist faction, the England cricket team was potentially a target.

There were moral concerns too, with Cook one of a number of players who felt a period of time without cricket – to allow the dead to be properly mourned – would be appropriate. (Interestingly, when terrorists had struck London's transport network three years earlier, England went ahead with a one-day international in Leeds, starting a couple of hours later on the same day.)

England scrapped the last two one-day internationals and left for Abu Dhabi while security was dialled up in India. They then returned for the two Test matches. Strauss clearly did not mind being overlooked for the captaincy, scoring brilliant centuries in each innings of the first of those Tests played in Chennai. England passed three hundred twice but the bowlers were unable to defend a target of 387 on the final day, India winning by six wickets thanks to an outstanding innings from Tendulkar. The second Test in Mohali was drawn. Cook's scores in that series were 50, 9, 50, 10. He featured in one stand with Strauss worth 118 and another with Pietersen of 103. England had performed with credit but India had won the series which, given how much everyone had been so deeply affected by the events in Mumbai, seemed appropriate.

Everyone went home for Christmas for some important rest ahead of what would be another big year in 2009 featuring thirteen Tests (including the small matter of the first home Ashes series since the nonpareil summer of 2005). Or that, anyway, was the intention.

However, the players had scarcely worked their way through their leftover turkey and cleared away the tinsel when a series of juddering tremors rocked the foundations of the elite game to its core.

On 7 January 2009, and just three Tests into his reign as captain, Pietersen tendered his resignation to the England

and Wales Cricket Board. What is certain is that he only did so because Hugh Morris, managing director of the England team, was convinced that Pietersen's captaincy style was so disliked by a majority of the England players that it was not tenable to have him in the position for any longer.

The ins and outs over who backed who, and whether or not Pietersen had any support at all among the senior players, were never really unearthed fully. The lingering issue of Pietersen's severe personality clash with the England dressing-room culture, and in particular his relationship with Cook, would resurface a few years later with a much messier outcome. For now, Pietersen very much stayed as a player in all formats but he would never again lead an England side across any of the three formats, and Strauss was the new Test captain.

More or less simultaneously, Peter Moores was sacked. He had failed to establish a working relationship with Pietersen and was deemed to be at least partially responsible for that chasm between the pair developing. In addition, England had lost four of the seven Test series they had contested under Moores, and that was considered highly unsatisfactory.

Later, Andy Flower was named as coach for the immediate tour of the Caribbean and would gradually prove his worth – certainly in the Test arena – to bed in for a long innings in that important role. England had been given the opportunity to start afresh, although they did so in a chaotic manner. As the new captain, Strauss had to find a way to control Pietersen's return to the ranks. Cook's autobiography slightly glosses over this period. Perhaps revealing a non-confrontational aspect to his character, he insists: 'I had no idea things were so bad between Pietersen and Moores. There had been no signs of real friction when we were in India.'

Like a number of observers – because that's what he felt he was in this peculiar situation, despite being an established member of the team – Cook felt the few days leading up to 7 January had been reduced into a survival contest between Moores and Pietersen, and that if one should go and one should stay, his money was on the captain appointed amid some degree of fanfare not many months previously.

In *Starting Out*, Cook is mildly critical of Pietersen's opinions about Moores reaching the public domain. Never one to operate with any degree of restraint or subtlety, Pietersen simply felt Moores had inadequate skills to perform his job competently, and through briefings – some of which were probably triggered by his management team – he made sure the media knew.

'Once that opinion got into the public domain, it caused a terrible crisis,' Cook wrote. 'It was the last thing we needed at the start of an Ashes career.'

Fortunately, as is always the way with a national cricket team, the next tour was around the corner, a chance to blow away the sour atmosphere, and the Caribbean is usually a pretty good place to head to as a suitable place to refocus the mind.

Cook's added focus came in his elevation to the vice-captaincy. In cricket, it is a largely ceremonial position though the incumbent is essentially earmarked as the likeliest stand-in if required – and potentially the next permanent captain.

In terms of being top dog, Cook was now 100 per cent behind the decision to appoint Strauss. He had, you will remember, idly wondered if England might give him the captaincy after Vaughan's resignation the previous summer. Presumably the latest crisis had focused his mind, or perhaps with Pietersen out of the way and being named vice-captain, Cook could begin to see an avenue to the future captaincy and, for now, concentrating on scoring runs was probably best for him and England in any case.

England performed desperately badly in Kingston, Jamaica, the first Test under the new regime. They were blown away for a pathetic fifty-one in their second innings to lose by an innings. The second Test, on a flat wicket in Antigua, provided runs galore for England but Cook was infuriated to get out in both innings soon after passing fifty. In all, fourteen Tests had passed since his tremendous century in Galle and he was due another century.

'My problem was more mental than technical,' he concluded. 'I was so desperate to reach three figures again, I had started to beat myself up about it. Maybe I was trying too hard. It's that bar of soap thing – the more desperate you become to cling on to it, the more likely it is to squeeze out of your hand.' In this period, for whatever reason, he did not find that calmness and poise that personifies Alastair Cook at the crease. Who knows? The turmoil caused by the resignation of Vaughan, and then Moores and Pietersen too, may have played its part. In later years, Cook would find it harder to get to fifty than he did in 2008 and early 2009, but when he did he tended to get the three-figure score.

When England got to Barbados for the third Test for four in the West Indies, they were still 1-0 down in the series with the home side having valiantly clung on to avoid defeat with their last pair. (It was every bit as frustrating as the Lord's draw with India two years earlier.)

The pitch presented in Bridgetown, perhaps to help West Indies preserve their precious series lead, was about as spiteful as a cuddly toy. Bowlers on both sides hated it. For a batsman desperate for a big score this was a good thing and Cook, after miscuing a hook shot on ninety-four in the first innings, had another opportunity to find the deliverance of a Test match century, and he got there on the final day with 139 not out. Trinidad was another draw and England, even if they had lost the series, were beginning to feel good about their batting unit. Strauss, with 541 runs at an average of 67.42, showed that if he hadn't quite picked up the winning thread as captain then he wasn't allowing the role to affect his batting in the slightest. Cook, Collingwood, Pietersen and Matt Prior were also in the runs. Now for the summer season at home – West Indies (again) and then Australia – and, it was hoped, some match-winning performances from bowlers who would appreciate sportier home wickets.

CHAPTER NINE

THE ASHES RECLAIMED

Some of the drama of the 2005 Ashes series, which is impossible to reference without drawing on one superlative after another – all of which are merited, by the way – is described in the introduction to this book. When 2009 began, the feeling was that a competitive series would be played as Australia's great champions of the era had retired and the new team, captained by Michael Clarke, was a strange mixture of older players who had finally been granted their chance and younger ones who were raw round the edges.

It was too much to expect 2005 revisited, but a keenly fought battle that would pay tribute to the great legacy of Ashes cricket was in the offing. But first, a prelude as England played West Indies again.

In the period of West Indies domination (loosely 1975–1995) England struggled to lay a glove on a team with superstars like Viv Richards, Michael Holding, Gordon Greenidge and Malcolm Marshall in it.

Since then, and up to the present day, England have tended to dominate the home series against West Indies while finding themselves frustrated on foreign soil. This was very much the shape of things in 2009 because the short two-match rubber in May ended in a 2-0 verdict to England. It was extremely important, after all the internal squabbling in the New Year and the series defeat in the West Indies, that Strauss's team began to assert itself once again and move back towards the top of the Test ladder.

Cook's 160 in the second Test at Chester-le-Street showed that Bridgetown had been no fluke. Instead, it was the catalyst that provided self-belief once again; he had rediscovered his innate ability to bat for lengthy periods of time. Cook batted throughout the first day up in Durham where Jerome Taylor, the same bowler who had mown down the England top order in Jamaica, was rendered impotent.

On day one in Durham, he put on 213 in partnership with Ravi Bopara, his long-term Essex teammate going back to their schooldays. When Bopara was out, James Anderson, Cook's best friend in the squad, came out for the last few overs. It made Cook very happy that he spent the vast majority of his day batting with these two.

Writing in *The Guardian*, Vic Marks, one of the most intelligent observers of the game, offered grudging admiration: 'The sprinkling of spectators, huddling together for warmth, seemed distinctly under-awed. Runs from Cook do not necessarily help. He is an admirable cricketer, a precocious one even. Who has a better record for England at the tender age of twenty-four?

'Statistically, he probably outstrips David Gower at this stage of his career. But whereas Gower somehow had the capacity to entice someone to cross the Pennines on a pushbike on the off-chance that a silky half-century might be witnessed, you would barely cross the A167 in Chester-le-Street in a four-wheel drive to watch Cook. A cover-drive from Cook travels the same speed and distance as that of Gower's all those years ago. But we don't gasp. After forty-three Tests, Cook has never been dropped, a distinction he shares with Kevin Pietersen in this team, but no one else. That indignity is not imminent. He is one of the foundations of the side but we will appreciate him even more when he scores ugly runs against Australia in July.'

This book has already touched on the aspect of Cook as a great producer of runs, without supplying the style points that please the punters. The point barely requires labouring. Yet is there a point at which cricket's long-term sustainability as an entertainment product depends on its practitioners considering the manner in which they go about their business? It is, after all, competing with so many other pursuits for the leisure pound. Perhaps the most reasonable conclusion to draw is that a well-balanced team will have in it enough flair players to satisfy the PR people and that the diligent, and aesthetically blessed technicians should just be left to get on with it.

England were very happy to let Cook get on with it when the Ashes started, but he – and the team as a whole – fluffed their lines somewhat alarmingly in the series opener in Cardiff and came within a hair's breadth of losing it on the final day.

When the rain came six overs after tea on day three, Australia were 479-5 in reply to England's 435 and a draw looked very likely. But the Aussies piled on a barrage of runs on the fourth day, declaring on 674-6 and then dismissing Cook and Bopara before stumps.

A very painful final day for everyone ensued. Australia's bowlers kept taking wickets at one end, but couldn't shift Collingwood until the game was almost in its final thrashings. That left the final-wicket pair, Anderson and Panesar, to survive thirty-five minutes. Somehow they did just that in a finish every bit as absorbing as those at Edgbaston, Old Trafford and Trent Bridge back in 2005, and the teams headed off to Lord's all square.

Strauss won the toss at HQ and England batted first, racking up 364-6 on the first day. His own eighteenth Test century was a truly masterful one but he set the tone with Cook (ninety-five) in what was England's highest opening Ashes stand since 1991. The 196 runs they put on were scored in less than forty-eight overs, an extraordinarily fast rate for an opening partnership in an English Test match. What it showed was this: for all their personal difficulties in finding success in one-day internationals, Strauss and Cook were pretty merciless at dealing with poor bowling. On that day, the Australians were wayward too often, and when they strayed in line they were put away.

This Test was a fine one to attend as an England fan. After so many problems trying to capture the right balance in the bowling, that department was beginning to fire. Anderson and Broad were beginning to gel as a combination, Flintoff was still inspirational in his final Test series and Graeme Swann proved he possessed the right appetite for the big occasion.

The Edgbaston Test was severely curtailed by a Midlands monsoon, and then came Leeds with everyone in the home camp feeling positive, holding a 1-0 lead. Inexplicably, it all went Pete Tong in Yorkshire. 'It really was an awful Test for us,' wrote Cook. 'We were beaten so badly that a lesser side could have been irreparably damaged.'

Pietersen missed that match as he required an urgent Achilles operation, which also ruled him out of the upcoming decider at the Oval. With Bopara's form deserting him, England now called up Jonathan Trott for the final Test. It was an inspired pick.

Trott bats similarly to Cook. A fierce determination, unusually powerful reserves of concentration, exceptionally well coached and technically adept, Trott would make the number three position his own during the course of the next few seasons, though it was at five where he slotted in for the decider.

Trott hit an important 41 in the first innings and 119 in the second to ensure England had control of the match. However, in order to wrest back the urn from the pesky Aussies, a drawn match (and series) would not be good enough.

It required one more good day with the ball to seal the series, and England found it. Swann and Steve Harmison, in his final Test, shared the wickets – though Broad was the deserved Man of the Match for his impressive burst on the second afternoon. And Cook? He took the catch that won the series, stuffed it in his pocket and keeps it as a souvenir on his mantelpiece.

He acknowledged afterwards: 'It had not been the greatest of series for me with the bat, but that could not take any of the gloss off the achievement as far as I was concerned.' Cook had a long chat with one of Australia's best batsmen, Michael Hussey, after the series. He was advised not to worry about any lean spells and trust in the methods that had got him to where he was. He signed off *Starting Out* by asserting: 'I am confident that, with hard work, there will be plenty more runs again in the future. I also know there is a long and exciting journey ahead for us if we are to progress to being the best team in the world. I very much want to be part of that journey. The good times, I hope, have only just begun.'

Cook had now played Test cricket in England, India, Australia, Sri Lanka, New Zealand and West Indies. He had not yet experienced a tour to South Africa, and now was his moment to reach that particular milestone.

Since post-apartheid re-admission to the international fold in 1992, South Africa and England have tended to be extremely closely matched, ensuring some tremendous cricket with plenty of memorable encounters. Unusually, and it may be because the nature of the wickets in both countries is not too dissimilar, neither side tends to boast much of an advantage at home.

England had won on their previous tour of South Africa, but then been beaten at home by Graeme Smith's men – the series in which Vaughan tendered his resignation.

Cook's batting average during 2009 had fluctuated between what would be an all-time career low of 40.87, after the first Test in the West Indies, to a healthy 45.02 three months later. Since then, it had declined somewhat to 42.79. Traditionally, a batsman is judged an extremely competent one in the Test arena if he can maintain an average in the forties, and truly exceptional if he can end his career in the fifties.

Virat Kohli (53.38), Kane Williamson (52.88), and Cheteshwar Pujara (51.18) are the only current players averaging in excess of 50. It is highly likely that Steve Smith, whose year-long ban for ball-tampering has now expired, will return to the Australia side with a spectacular average of 61.37.

None of them are openers, who have it tougher as they always face fresh bowling, fresh wickets and hard new balls that bounce more, swing more and seam more. In other words, a Test average in the forties is what any opener should happily aspire to and Cook would need a solid series in South Africa to stay in that bracket.

South Africa had a very good bowling attack, however. Dale Steyn, accurate and skiddy, Makhaya Ntini, relentless and experienced, Morne Morkel, tall and awkward, were all categorised in the fast bracket. Then there were the batsmen – Smith, Amla, Kallis, De Villiers.

England's home defeat of Australia had ended that country's long run as the best Test team on official rankings and promoted South Africa as the new top dogs. Interestingly, they held that mantle for just three months. By the time England turned up in the land of biltong and diamonds, India held control of the ICC Test Championship mace. A convincing series win against Strauss's men would go a long way in wresting it back for a longer tenure, however.

England in South Africa proved to be another memorable series. In the opener in Centurion, despite one or two good individual performances, England were just not quite as good as South Africa, but a draw seemed assured when they were just three wickets down at tea on the final day. Then Pietersen ran himself out on eighty-one, the unheralded Friedel de Wet took three quick wickets, and once Broad and Swann had also come and gone it was left to Graham Onions to see off the final over. He just about managed it, and England had scraped the draw.

By sharp contrast, the Boxing Day Test at Durban was one of the great England away-from-home performances of the decade. After two weather-affected days, it was an even contest but Cook's tenth career century helped England establish a 234-run lead on first innings, and on the last two days Broad and Swann were irresistible. England had beaten the best team in Test cricket, on their own patch, in four days by an innings.

Cook's 118 was actually eclipsed by Ian Bell's 140, but by occupying six hours and forty minutes at the top of the order, Cook had worn out the bowlers and helped establish the groundwork for Bell's pretty embellishment – the Peter Beardsley to Bell's Gary Lineker, if you like. The fairly novel decision review system – allowing batsmen to challenge any decisions perceived to be erroneous – played its part when Cook was given out, caught at short leg on sixty-four. He appealed the decision and had it reversed.

When it was time to assess his career as a whole, Cook's record against South Africa, who have never put out a weak bowling attack, left a little to be desired, but not on this occasion. Rob Bagchi's assessment in the *Daily Telegraph* of Cook's ten best Test innings places this at number nine. He writes:

'Cook's first of only two Test centuries in eighteen Tests against South Africa, his most difficult opponents, was a nuggety masterpiece against Morne Morkel, Makhaya Ntini and Dale Steyn, and one which he attributed to the dedication of England's newly appointed batting consultant, Graham Gooch. Until a late assault on the spinner Paul Harris, Cook frustrated the bowlers by rotating the strike with a series of pokes, prods, shovelly flicks and tucks. It was a technique that looked manufactured and iffy and a thoroughbred such as Steyn could be forgiven for thinking it spawny. But it took great skill as well as grit to work the angles and grind the bowlers down until they played to his strengths.'

Cook himself, and not for the first time, insisted all the credit lay with Gooch for helping him compile that score. 'Goochie's almost worked harder to change my technique than I have,' he told the Durban press pack.

'He will think nothing of throwing balls for an hour and a half, three times a week, and that's a lot of hard work. I have changed my trigger movements but it takes time to settle that in, to groove it. It's nowhere near finished. But this innings will give me a lot of confidence.

'I'm delighted and relieved. It's a little milestone to get my tenth Test century as well. In the last few games the side have been playing really well and I haven't really contributed. I feel I've been carried by my teammates, so it's nice to repay that back to them.

'I've never been the prettiest batsman to watch. In the first hour I got about one. It was nice to get my patience working, to get through that period and to get rewarded later in the day. Just after the Ashes series I experimented in the last month of the season with Essex and changed a few things.

'I scored a couple of one-day hundreds. It was trial and error but it's nice to know I'm on the right track. I was pleased with my discipline today. It could have all ended in tears. But I didn't even flirt with one ball all morning. It's good for my confidence to know that I can do that.'

Cook had everybody he needed around him to develop his game at the precise phase in his career that he was ready to take the next step – to raise his average, score centuries more regularly, become the lynchpin of the England batting order. Gooch, who had devoted so much time to Cook in the winter after he had left school, was part of the England circle now. This was a huge bonus for Cook. Flower, the teammate he had looked up in his first days at Essex, who himself had also acted as an England batting coach, headed the coaching set-up at a national level.

Having just turned twenty-five, still a young man with many miles left to run on the clock, Cook was fortunate that things tended to work out for him. Perhaps he deserved it. When someone told Gary Player that he was 'lucky' the great golfer replied: 'That's funny, the more I practise, the luckier I get.' It's a phrase that coaches often use today to hammer home the importance of hard graft. Those that listen often do better than their peers. In the Manchester United Academy in the early 1990s, the player who stayed practising free kicks at the Cliff long after every other kid had gone home was David Beckham. Seve Ballesteros used to fall asleep in class having played clandestine rounds of golf on his own at La Pedrena until it got dark. Steve Redgrave and Matthew Pinsent did not wear watches when training together in the run-up to the Olympics. They had an alarm at home that went at 6.30am; they headed straight to the river and when it got dark it was time to head home. They only realised they had got to the weekend when the river was busier than the other days.

Just like them, Cook wanted to work all the time. As a batsman, you do need someone else feeding the bowling machines, or chucking balls at you from twelve yards. Fortunately, Cook tended to have Gooch there.

England showed plenty of resilience in the third Test of the series in South Africa, the traditional New Year contest at beautiful Newlands, Cape Town. They had to bat for more than ten hours to rescue a draw, which they managed – just about. Once again, they were nine wickets down at the end. In the history of Test cricket, there have only been twenty-two Tests drawn with one wicket remaining. At this point in his career, Cook had been involved in four of them. Incredibly, he would also feature in two more. To put this into further context, while only 0.09% of Test matches have been drawn with one wicket remaining, Cook has found himself in one of these matches in 3.7% of his own appearances.

By the time the players reached Johannesburg for the series wrap, England needed to steal another draw if they could, to emerge with a famous win in the rubber. To their credit, South Africa forced a dominant victory on this occasion, establishing a massive first-innings lead before bowling England out on the fourth day of a match severely curtailed by bad weather, to win by an innings and seventy-four runs. The lingering memory of that match is that England rather gave it away in their second innings. If they had only got to at least tea on day four they would have seen the rains return to wipe out the final four sessions of the match.

There were some wild swipes and swishes across the line – not by Cook one should add. Perhaps they had run out of energy.

It had been a fine series, all the same. In Cricinfo, Andrew Miller's 'marks out of ten' assessment of Cook's performances offered him a seven, behind only Collingwood and Swann.

Miller noted: 'He began the series with the vultures circling, and was conceivably in last-chance saloon going into the second Test, where he responded with a brilliant display of temperament over technique, as he left religiously outside off stump, and willed himself back to form in an indomitable six-and-a-half hour century. He carried that same mindset into the Cape Town rearguard before tailing off in the face of furious pace bowling at the Wanderers. But overall he has taken massive strides.'

CHAPTER TEN

A TASTE OF THE CAPTAINCY

Andrew Strauss had batted poorly in the Test series in South Africa over the 2009–2010 winter and in mid-January Geoff Miller, the national selector, announced he would be rested for the upcoming tour of Bangladesh.

'Andrew Strauss has provided outstanding leadership for the team in both forms of the game over the past twelve months and the selectors feel it is important that he takes a break ahead of an extremely busy programme of international cricket leading up to and including the Ashes series in Australia and the ICC Cricket World Cup in 2011,' read Miller's statement.

'Our decision to appoint Alastair Cook to the Test vice-captaincy last year clearly demonstrated the belief that he has the potential to be a future England captain. Alastair will now have an opportunity to develop his leadership skills still further by leading the side in both forms of cricket in Bangladesh and I know that he is excited by the challenge and looking forward to working closely with Andy Flower.'

And there we were. This was partially a case of Cook filling in for Strauss, but there was a little bit more nuance to the appointment. Miller's words brooked no doubt that Cook would essentially be featuring in a dress rehearsal. If the Bangladesh tour went well, Cook could pretty much look forward to being named England's permanent captain in due course. At the time, Strauss was approaching thirty-three while Cook had just turned twenty-five. Rather oddly, considering he had not played a single ODI in 2009, he was also appointed captain for the one-day international in Bangladesh.

The short-format games came first, England winning the series 3-0 with Cook in the runs and the Tests followed. Cook duly became the fifth England captain to score a hundred in his first match at the helm of the national team. Having only struck two sixes previously in his Test career, Cook hit two more in this innings alone, both slog-sweeps, in an innings oozing with confidence. The bowling started off modestly and got steadily poorer, but on slow Bangladeshi wickets batsmen always have to go hard at the ball to accrue runs and that's what he did.

Bangladesh, who had now been playing Tests for nearly ten years, were just beginning to transform themselves from permanent whipping-boys to genuine Test-level performers, having beaten West Indies twice away from home the previous year.

That meant England had to work reasonably hard to take twenty wickets in each of those Tests. Cook, as captain, needed to cajole the most he could out of a thin bowling attack with just four frontline options. Essentially, it meant Swann wheeling away at one end – he bowled nearly eighty overs in that first Test – and rotating the seamers at the other.

The second Test in Dhaka was a similar story, although this time there was, sensibly, a second spinner. Bangladesh were even harder to beat, scoring 419 in the first innings and then having England in a degree of difficulty at 174-4.

Bell, in tremendous form in this period, hit a gritty 138 and Tim Bresnan 91 to establish a healthy enough lead, whereupon England, after bowling better in the second innings, were ultimately set a target of 209 to win. Cook took on the challenge himself with a degree of gusto to secure his twelfth Test century in a very satisfactory nine-wicket win.

Before Cook could slip back into the ranks for the summer, it was time to assess how he had handled this first taste of captaincy. There were concerns that Bangladesh had been allowed to score too freely initially in their 419, and again towards the end of that same innings. When the bowlers came under pressure, Cook could have tried a few exploratory tactics but seemed content to stick with plans that were simply not working.

That aside, he had come back with 100 per cent winning record, and Swann was most complimentary afterwards. He said: 'I think Cooky's done an exceptional job. Coming here to Bangladesh, there is a pressure to win every match, and win convincingly. I think that's something that goes back over the last decade, from playing against teams that were weaker in the past. They are not a pushover any more. You have to play good hard cricket, you have to have a strong leader, and you have to have a cohesive unit. I think Cooky has been an exceptional leader under those circumstances.'

The rested Strauss duly returned to lead England for the whole of the 2010 summer, which started with two home Tests against Bangladesh and segued into four against Pakistan. Cook hit a minor bump in the road when failing to hit thirty in three innings against Bangladesh but England, nevertheless, cruised to their expected wins in those matches and then it was time for Pakistan.

This was a series that featured an extraordinary concluding contest at Lord's when the cricket went on amid lurid tabloid 'spot-fixing' revelations. It appeared that a sting operation, in which captain Salman Butt was the ringleader and bowlers Mohammad Asif and Mohammad Amir were instructed to bowl no-balls to order, had been exposed.

Leading the series 2-1 at that point, England were actually in deep trouble on the opening day at 102-7 before a 332-run stand between Trott and Broad, who both scored centuries, the latter batting at number nine. By the time the fixing operation had been exposed, Pakistan were already on the ropes in the match, managing just seventy-four in their first innings and deep into their follow-on. The match ended in decidedly muted fashion.

Cook had a slightly odd series, in that the one century he scored came in England's sole defeat, at the Oval. Up until that point, he had contributed a mere 106 runs in eight Test innings during the England summer. There always seemed to be a little build-up of worryingly lowish scores and then a blessed, relief-providing century for him in this period. It was almost like inside himself there was a mini stock market at play, with buy orders poised for those moments his average started dropping down into the low forties.

'You can get carried away with technique,' he said after that Oval century. 'I've had a lot of advice over the last couple of weeks, so I tried to go out and hit the ball and score some runs, and not worry so much about my feet and my backlift. I just tried to be more positive. Obviously the conditions allowed me to do that, they were quite tough at the top of the order, but I wasn't going to die wondering and that helped my defence.

'I've been feeling under pressure. When you are playing for England there's always pressure, and when you don't perform that multiplies a lot. But to respond like I did was very satisfying and showed some character. You don't know what it's like until you get into that situation, but it doesn't mean I'm out of the woods either. Even if you are in the best form ever, you've still got to work hard, and I'm going to keep doing that.'

CHAPTER ELEVEN

RUNS IN AUSTRALIA

This chapter, the most enjoyable one to write about Alastair Cook, starts with an almighty spoiler. The most runs ever scored by a batsman in a five-match Ashes series is 974 – by Don Bradman, of course. He got them in 1930 and his success during that English summer was one of the key reasons why, when Douglas Jardine took the captaincy for a tour of Australia two and a half years later, he resorted to controversial tactics – the 'Bodyline' series, it was called. The Don also features at number three in this list, when hitting 810 in the 1936–37 series. Best of the English is Wally Hammond, splitting Bradman's two series of plenty with a haul of 905 in 1928–29.

Until the 2010–11 Ashes, the remarkable Bradman also had the fourth highest aggregate. Then along came Cook, blitzing 766 in a landmark series both for him personally, and for a generation of long-suffering fans whose previous trips to Australia had provided scant cause for celebration. England had last tasted success in a Test series in Australia back in 1986–87 in the days of Ian Botham, Chris Broad and Gladstone Small.

In the five series staged down under since that memorable series, England had never even threatened to shock the Aussies in their back yard. The 'Poms' had just three Test wins to show for their efforts in that era; Australia had eighteen.

For the first time in a long while, there was genuine hope that things might be different this time for Andrew Strauss's men. England, after all, had won the last two Ashes series staged in England and if the 2009 Australians had a transitional look to them, then it was a similar story a year and a half later. Where there was a choice between an experienced but flawed player and young potential, the Australian selectors went with the first option. Almost thirty-six, Ricky Ponting no longer scared England. He was on the way down from the extraordinary heights he had reached, but retained the captaincy and the number three berth. Simon Katich and Shane Watson would open the batting even though neither man was a natural opener. In the middle order, Michael Clarke and Michael Hussey both began the series looking for a bit of form, and Marcus North was known to be vulnerable early in his innings. Then there was the wicketkeeper Brad Haddin and the bowlers. And it was the bowlers who were the real weakness for Australia. Hilfenhaus, Siddle, Johnson and Doherty – this was not a quartet to set shivers down the spine of English batsmen. Cook came to form at the right time too. He failed to reach ten in either innings against Western Australia in Perth, where the first of the three warm-up matches was played. At this point, one or two individuals in the media were again – and in retrospect this seems utterly ridiculous – considering whether his place in the Tests might be under threat. However, an unbeaten century against South Australia and sixty against Australia A put an end to that rumour.

So it was rather disappointing for everyone when, after day one of the first Test in Brisbane, England found themselves in decidedly familiar territory: winning a key toss but bowled out for 260. There was some loose shot-making. Strauss carelessly swatted the third ball of the match to gully, Trott and Pietersen fell to loose drives, and Cook was also culpable of contributing to his own demise. He had been dropped on twenty-six, slashing a wide, short delivery to point and with regular wickets falling at the other end it was essential he stayed there. Australia bowled well to him, barely feeding him anything short or on his pads, and eventually he pushed defensively at a delivery well wide of off stump that he should have left, nicking it to slip.

Cook's sixty-seven and Bell's seventy-six were the only half-centuries in the innings and England knew they had not done enough on a good batting wicket. When Australia responded with 481, Hussey starring with 195, they were really up against it.

The good thing with Brisbane is that unless the cracks on the surface come into play by providing variable bounce – and on this occasion they did not – conditions tend to remain reasonably comfortable for batting. The key is to overcome the new ball, and then just play the ball on its merits. Cook and Strauss did exactly that, batting together for 66 overs in a partnership of 188 in the second innings. England needed to go on, and they did; Trott came in and he and Cook took the score to 517 without a further wicket falling. Cook had struck 235 by then in ten and a half hours, Trott 135. The Australian fans hated it. The Barmy Army loved it. Strauss did not have to declare, but he did anyway to give all the bowlers a quick spell. And that was sensible – there are never quite enough warm-up games scheduled before the serious stuff begins and the second Test was just around the corner.

How good was Cook's 235? Certainly towards the end there were some exquisite, expansive, frankly un-Cook like shots. Before that, he had to be obviously a lot more circumspect. Australia continued to avoid bowling on Cook's legs, so in terms of release shots the early stage of the innings was marked by a variety of cut shots – some against the fast bowlers, some against the spin of Xavier Doherty, who he took a real liking to. There were just two false shots, a top-edge pull when he had reached 103, off Hilfenhaus, that almost carried to fine leg and an outside edge through a vacant second slop some time later.

The cover-drive off Watson to go to 174 and reach a new Test-best was a sweet strike, and, once the game was safe and he could really enjoy himself, there were two delightful sashays down the wicket to hammer Doherty straight for four. These shots were surely little tribute acts to Gooch, who loved skipping towards the slow bowlers and bludgeoning the ball back past them.

This marathon effort was ranked the second best of Cook's Test innings by the *Daily Telegraph*, whose Rob Bagchi described it thus:

'Given that England began their second innings 221 behind and with fears of the same old capitulation palpable, Cook's relentlessly positive innings was emblematic of England's confidence and fighting spirit. So adeptly did he blunt then punish Mitchell Johnson that the self-assurance of Australia's most devastating bowler fell apart ... Johnson took years to recover.'

A number of records were set by England in their second innings at Brisbane. Cook's 235 was the highest Test score at the Gabba, while the partnership of 329 between him and Trott was also a ground record. It was also the first time the top three in an England innings had hit centuries since 1924.

Tom Fordyce's BBC blog opined: 'At the start of the final day, there was a fear England could still lose. With a lead of just eighty-eight overnight, a rush of early wickets could have triggered a deathly slide. Instead, it was Australia who fell apart. First the wheels came off. Then the wing mirrors fell off, too, followed by the bumpers, then the doors. Ricky Ponting, like a modern-day Buster Keaton, was left sitting on the ground surrounded by the wreckage, steering wheel in his hands and an utterly bemused look on his face. It was like stepping into some surreal parallel universe, a dream-like place where everything was the exact opposite of what you had come to expect.'

In my own report for the BBC website, I suggested

'the intangible aspect of England's dominance over the last two days is what the effect might be on Australia'.

The answer to that casually pondered thought came through loud and clear on the morning of 3 December. A three-day break in a Test series is often barely enough time to refocus on tasks at hand, especially when there's a flight and a new hotel to throw into the mix. Australia had barely started proceedings at Adelaide before they found themselves battling to stay in contention.

A run-out in the first over meant James Anderson suddenly had his dander up against numbers three and four with a rock-hard ball – and he delivered: a golden duck for Ricky Ponting and a six-ball two for Michael Clarke left Australia 3-2 on one of the most inviting batting decks in world cricket. There was a partial recovery to 245, but there was no way England were going to let the Aussies off the hook in the way the hosts had done to them in Brisbane. The first key to maintaining their dominant position was to score big in the first innings. They did just that, and Cook was once again to the fore.

Utterly relishing the challenge laid down and feeding off the confidence he had found in Brisbane, Cook hit another century, this time with Pietersen for company, and at stumps on day two he was on 136 with England 317-2. Things were going just swimmingly. Fortunately for Cook, he was not swimming in his own sweat as that would have made gripping the bat difficult.

It was something that was picked up on in the press conference after that day's play, which had been conducted in heat hovering up close to 40 degrees Celsius.

By this point, he had spent almost seventeen hours at the crease and scored a record 371 unbeaten runs since taking guard in the second innings of the first Test at the Gabba the previous week. Yet clearly, batting for these exceptionally long periods provided nothing but pleasure for him – there was no mental or physical toil. It was all inspiration, without perspiration.

'I'm quite lucky – I don't really sweat that much,' he said. 'I only wore one pair of gloves all day, while Kev was changing them every other over. I'm built in a way that I don't get too hot and don't really sweat – so it was all right.

'It was excellent conditions to bat in – 37 degrees Celsius on a very good wicket. At tea, I was quite tired. It's up there with the hottest days I've ever played cricket on. We've toured some hot places. We're accustomed to it. As Goochie says: "You've got to cash in when you're in this kind of form – don't give it away." There was no chance of doing that. But yes, it was physically quite hard after what happened last week as well.

'I don't think I'm doing anything differently. You put in all the hard yards and then you get little rewards, like I've had this week. It's important to enjoy them when you get them, but remember there's a lot of hard work to come. If you ever need a reminder of how quickly cricket changes, you only have to look at me last summer.'

Under those cloudy skies in Trent Bridge and Edgbaston, against Pakistani bowlers capable of exploiting the assistance that came their way, Cook had certainly struggled, prodding about uncertainly, and he did not have any problem reminding those reporters in Adelaide about the facts.

'I think I scored a hundred runs in seven knocks. You guys wouldn't have been doing your job if you hadn't criticised me. How I dealt with it – by responding at the Oval – has given me a lot of confidence that when I really needed it most I could deliver.'

All those hours of extra fitness work were really beginning to pay off. Cook was not unusual in tending to find life easier when the sun was out. What did make him different was that he never allowed extreme heat to compromise him. There have been plenty of instances through the years of a good batsman with his eye in on a good track who has eventually lost his wicket through cramp, heat exhaustion, or dehydration. Sometimes, the concentration just begins to waver a little. Tiredness affects the focus and then – bam! – it's all over. Cook was not like that, particularly in the Ashes series of 2010–11. He was ruthless, lethal and unforgiving in equal measure.

Cricket had become increasingly professionalised over the years, and there were three key historical events that have allowed players to climb steeply up the pay-grade ladder. Before the first of them, it was barely a professional sport at all.

The first of these events was the most seismic of all and came when Kerry Packer spied an opportunity to launch his World Series Cricket in the late 1970s. This was an era when televised sport was becoming a big deal. Football had Pelé, Beckenbauer and Cruyff. Tennis had Borg and Connors. The Olympics produced Nadia Comăneci. Boxing, of course, had Muhammad Ali.

Cricket was missing out, and Packer, who owned the cash-rich Nine Network, was frustrated at being snubbed repeatedly with his generous bids to stage and promote Test cricket. So he simply signed up a number of the game's top players to take part in a non-official cricket league which was heavily marketed and successful enough to threaten the establishment in such a way as to trigger a total transformation in the way administrators dealt with broadcasters. The big winners, ultimately, were the players.

The next change was central contracts, wherein players became employees of the national board rather than their domestic teams. Obviously, this varied from country to country, but in England the year 2000 was the significant moment when elite players stopped getting a county retainer with England fees paid on top. Significantly, Australia had done the same thing six years earlier and immediately reaped results.

Finally, and in quite a gradual way, there has been the beginnings of a movement towards 'free agent' status. Some of the most skilful cricketers across the world are actually choosing to forgo Test cricket altogether. They might still play some international cricket, but on a reduced basis, in order to take advantage of the lucrative opportunities in the various Twenty20 leagues popping up all over the world.

In the 2010–11 season this was not yet a realistic avenue. However, Alastair Cook was firmly a professional cricketer of the post-Packer, post-central contract. As such, he would have been well looked after on a central England contract but the fall from that level back into county ranks is a sharp one, and he had already needed to haul himself once or twice from potentially heading that way.

If you needed to invent a job with a natural key performance indicator attached to it, then professional cricket would be that job. The runs you score and the wickets you take are the very currency that establishes your value to the firm (well, team in this case).

That is why Cook's century in Bridgetown in February 2009, which stopped his average sliding below forty, and the one at the Oval in August 2010, ending another run of low scores, were so important. Effectively, they kept him firmly within the bracket of top-tier central contract-holders and the longer he could stay there, the less likely he was to drop out. Now, with this deluge of runs in Australia, he was beginning to reach a status at which it would be very hard for anyone to ever drop him.

England duly won the second Test to establish a 1-0 lead in the Ashes – an away Ashes, ye Gods! – and Cook was feted as the run-machine that had put England in this most exciting position. It was at this point that Donald McRae caught up with him for a fascinating interview published in *The Guardian*.

In it, Cook recounts a story in which a boy, perhaps fourteen, intercepted him in the aisle of his local supermarket in England earlier that year. The lad plucked up the courage to ask him 'You're Alastair Cook, aren't you?' When Cook nodded, he looked him up and down and had the temerity to say, 'You're not batting very well, are you?'

McRae asks Cook if he was 'tempted to give the mouthy squirt a clip.' Cook responds: 'I don't think I was too rude to him. But I didn't hang around either. We didn't have a conversation. It sent my blood pressure rocketing because you think, "Aw, what a little shit – what right has he got to say that?"'

It must, indeed, have been very hard not to be unnerved by the experience. It must have rankled with Cook and irritated him. Why would a fourteen-year-old boy choose to see the negative in somebody who was, essentially, a role model?

McRae's article notes that 'Cook might restrict himself to a narrow range of emotions stretching from the wooden to the mechanical in a typical press conference, where he talks with the same lack of flourish with which he bats, but here he is open and involving as he discusses his strangely turbulent year.' Cook revealed: 'I try not to read the papers but, naturally, it gets back to you. So in the summer I felt under huge pressure. It was, without doubt, the lowest time in my Test career. I've never been under the microscope like that – with people calling for my head.'

Cook responded to being wrong-footed in the supermarket by

scoring his Oval century. And yet not even that innings prevented various experts suggesting that England's Ashes campaign should begin with the axing of Cook.

'There was talk, quite rightly, because I hadn't had the greatest summer or the best record against Australia,' Cook told McRae. 'But I felt I deserved my place. We measure our annual stats from September 2009 to this September, and even before the Oval I was averaging over forty with three Test hundreds – one in Durban and two against Bangladesh. But it's amazing how quickly the game bites you in the arse.'

Another tremendous vignette is buried in the McRae piece. Cook and Sachin Tendulkar, of all people, quite by chance, had happened to dine in the same London restaurant one night before the Ashes tour – this fact was revealed to the journalist by Tendulkar. Cook says in the interview: 'I didn't want to badger him for long. It's surprising he spoke about me because, with Ricky Ponting, he's the greatest batsman I've ever seen. He probably had thirty Test centuries when he was twenty-five.'

Well, here's the thing: Tendulkar actually scored his twenty-first Test century a few weeks before his twenty-sixth birthday. Cook, about to turn twenty-six himself, had now hit fifteen to stand joint second alongside Don Bradman and behind the Indian in this particular hit parade. That is some trio.

Australia freshened up their team, stuck in some younger faces, guys like Phillip Hughes and Steve Smith, and recovered their mojo in Perth. They thumped England at the Western Australian Cricket Association (WACA) ground even though the match looked very even an hour into the second day. All out for just 268, Australia were still looking to break the now formidable Strauss-Cook opening partnership and once it reached seventy-eight, England could arguably be said to have had their noses in front.

But then it went wrong. Cook reached out to play a big drive against Mitchell Johnson and the ball took a thick edge out to Michael Hussey at gully, who gleefully collected the catch.

England then collapsed badly, to 98-5 and 187 all out. Australia suddenly held the aces and built up a big lead of 390 by the time their second innings came to an end. England's batsmen crumbled once again, alarmingly so in fact, to be dismissed for just 123. Cook's dismissal off the first ball of the seventh over was a particularly odd one, playing back to a full-length ball from the paceman Ryan Harris – precisely the sort of error he would never normally make.

Another classic Ashes series was brewing. England had worked so hard to obtain a crucial lead. Now they had meekly relinquished it. Cook (thirty-two and thirteen) had failed in both innings at the one ground he had mastered on his first England tour of Australia.

What it meant was that the traditional fourth Test on Boxing Day would be what the Aussies would call 'a ripper'. Normally the place where England begin to have the last rites read to them in an Ashes series, this would be an altogether different experience. England needed to draw on everything they had achieved at Brisbane and Adelaide and then perhaps all would be well, but some of the players wore the deep scars of the 5-0 whitewash four years previously. Cook was one of them.

On the day after his twenty-sixth birthday, Cook would have been an interested spectator peering from the players' balcony at the iconic Melbourne Cricket Ground when Strauss won the toss and went straight on the attack, making Australia bat first. It was a bold tactic, because the failure to take wickets early on a wicket that started with a greenish tinge but was likely to dry rapidly, could spell trouble.

England's bowlers were bang on the money from the word go. Even with Stuart Broad and Steven Finn both injured, the seamers proved irresistible. The tourists could even afford to drop Shane Watson twice before removing him in the fourth over. Then they tumbled like a pack of cards. Australia were all out for ninety-eight. On Boxing Day. In Melbourne. It was their second lowest score ever at the ground on which they had played their first Test way back in 1877. Anderson and Tremlett bowled in exhilarating style and complemented each other superbly. Tremlett, a tall, rapid and athletic bowler who was unfortunate not to play more Test cricket, made the ball bounce alarmingly from a good length. Anderson bowled like Anderson just does, probing away and getting that late swing that makes him so effective. He has never had express pace but is such a gifted technician that it has proved no obstacle to his sustained success and, by dint of that, he has enjoyed unusual longevity as a fast bowler in international cricket. All four of Anderson's wickets were little nicks to wicketkeeper Matt Prior.

Precariously placed at 1-1 in the series that very morning, England were suddenly a couple more good sessions away from exerting a stranglehold, not only on the fourth Test, but on the Ashes itself. Ensure victory in Melbourne and Sydney would be, to some extent, a dead rubber given that as Ashes holders England would retain the famous little urn in the event of a drawn series.

A good performance from England's fiercely on-form top order could leave Australia in the dust. So what transpired? Exactly that – a superbly controlled, disciplined and organised response which almost killed off the match as a viable contest at the end of day one. Even fortune favoured Strauss's team – the clouds that had helped England's bowlers melted away almost magically at the precise time Australia took to the field.

England went to bed on 157-0, already miles past Australia, with Strauss and Cook having seen off the new ball and hungry to bat on and on and on through the next day.

For English journalists, the temptation to gloat was almost irresistible. Lawrence Booth just about held on to his composure to write in the *Daily Mail*: 'So much for momentum. Jubilant in Adelaide, then pummelled in Perth, England today wrapped one finger round the urn with a performance of utter dominance and dollops of skill at the MCG. If the Boxing Day Test is the Australian sporting calendar's sacred cow, then their batsmen committed heresy in totalling ninety-eight.'

England's players were surprised by reaching such a dominant position going into day two. Anderson said: 'We've been good at bouncing back strongly, so we didn't expect anything less – but to do it so emphatically probably wasn't on the cards. 'It's an amazing feeling.'

In truth, England had been unsettled by the extra bounce in Perth. The drop-in pitch at the MCG – where the turf is pre-prepared and lifted into place – proved much more to their liking. These surfaces have a habit of taking a while to settle down. Once they do, conditions can be very pleasant for batting. But there is often a period, when the root structure has not yet bedded into the subsoil, when bowlers are able to hold sway if they adopt a disciplined approach.

'When we bowled them out it was very similar to English conditions, not a great deal of pace in the pitch but a little bit of sideways movement which is always nice,' Anderson said.

'We didn't over-attack, all the catches seemed to be going to first and second slip and the keeper, so the need for a third slip wasn't there, we put him at extra-cover and it worked brilliantly for us.'

This was an unusual tactic from Strauss. The perceived wisdom when you are on the attack is to leave a gap at extra-cover to encourage the drive and hope to pick up edges to the slips. By positioning an extra-cover, Strauss gave Anderson, Tremlett and Tim Bresnan licence to bowl the ball full on off stump in the knowledge that a man was positioned to stop the easy single pushed into the covers, or even the full-blooded drives unless they were perfectly placed.

Thousands of Australians elected to head to the beach or fire up the barbie on day two, or just do anything rather than be at the cricket to witness another likely mauling. With only the Barmy Army (of course), a few tiny pockets of home supporters, and the media to bear witness, Cook added just two runs to his overnight score to depart for eighty-two. It needed a really good ball from Siddle to do it, pitching on middle and angling away with a bit of movement off the seam to carry to second slip. After another eleven runs, Strauss joined his opening partner back in the pavilion. They had done their jobs, however, and big scores from Trott (168), Prior (85) and Pietersen (51) took England out of sight with a total of 513 and a lead of 415. Australia now faced an impossible task to wrest back the Ashes and England completed the formalities to close out the win early on the fourth day.

Sydney was a chance to add some extra polish to what had already been a series to remember. Clearly a 3-1 scoreline would look more attractive than 2-1, and certainly a lot more satisfactory than 2-2, even though any of the three would ensure the Ashes remained in England's mitts. This time Australia chose to bat first and did a little better with the bat without ever hitting top gear, and it was odd watching players representing this proud nation scoring at barely two runs an over, which is what happened on the opening day. There was a little more energy at the back end of the innings but a total of 280 was below optimum.

Cook and Strauss put on another outstanding opening partnership in response. Frankly, Hilfenhaus, Johnson and Siddle must have been growing sick of the sight of these two left-handers batting with so much skill, composure, concentration and certainty. Strauss rattled along rapidly, with sixty off fifty-eight balls, while Cook cruised at Cook pace. Unbeaten on sixty-one at the end of day two, he almost batted the whole of day three as well. There must have been many times that Australian summer when somebody would have come back from work to open a beer, flop on the sofa, flick on the TV and think 'Strewth, not Cook again.' Conversely, the keen *Test Match Special* aficionados back home, huddling under their duvet on a cold winter's night, would have drifted in and out of sleep, hearing the name Cook repeated at regular intervals, and inwardly smiled.

On this occasion, he scored 189 off 342 balls in a 488-minute stay at the crease. There was one major slice of luck, when he looked for all the world to have been caught at mid-on off the rookie spinner Michael Beer when on forty-six. But umpire Billy Bowden made use of a brand-new loophole that afforded a greater deal of flexibility to officials when it came to adjudging no-balls, and particularly when a batsman was dismissed off a potential no-ball. On this occasion, Australia were already celebrating the wicket when Bowden informed the players that he was going to ask the third umpire to check the landing position of Beer's front foot when he bowled the ball. Replays provided enough evidence to show no part of Beer's heel was behind the line. By this time Cook was within a few yards of walking over the boundary line, with Kevin Pietersen rushing out to explain what was going on. Cook slightly sheepishly wandered back to the crease to resume his innings.

Australia weren't happy, but nowadays this system is almost commonplace. Back then it was a novelty and players were adapting to it in much the same way that footballers are trying to get used to the VAR system as it is belatedly introduced across the major leagues, cups and international tournaments.

There were no alarms after that. Cook played some outstanding pull shots in this innings, picking up the length exceptionally early and hitting invariably in front of square, in zones unoccupied by catchers. Australia had bowled too short to Cook in Melbourne and frequently erred that way again. It was death by a thousand cuts for Australia – or at least a dozen or so, frequently hit confidently over gully's head for four.

There were also three divine leg-glances hit fine for four off the seamers where he showed an unusually delicate touch and a pull shot off Siddle that was contemptuous, a seriously muscular blow hit over midwicket, and early in the innings too. This was a batsman in exceptionally confident form.

Even once Cook was out, Australia's bowlers were kept out in the field for several hours of extra torment. Bell, slightly more patient but just as impressive, hit a century off his own. So did Prior, a merciless 118 off 130 balls. In their second innings, Australia were bowled out for 281, to lose by an innings and 83 runs. England had won the Ashes. There had been spectacular performances from so many Englishmen through the past weeks, reward for the sweat, toil and sheer hard work they had put in, deliverance from so many bad experiences in Australia over the years. There were heroes everywhere – James Anderson, so often a shadow of himself on overseas tours, came away with twenty-four wickets and never bowled a spell that did not ask serious questions of the opposition. There was depth to England's seam-bowling strength too. Chris Tremlett, only playing because Stuart Broad got injured, took seventeen in three matches. Tim Bresnan, only playing because Steven Finn got injured, took eleven in two. Every batsman in the top six hit at least one century and all except Strauss averaged in excess of fifty. Jonathan Trott was terrific with 445 runs at an average of eighty-nine. Andy Flower could also say he was the first England coach since Micky Stewart to win an away Ashes series, and the fact he almost melted into the background says everything about his quiet but oh-so-effective style. He did not waste words and whatever he told the players between Perth and Melbourne, whatever he did to ensure their confidence levels remained high, worked ten-fold. Flower was also a deceptively hard-nosed character, but without distancing himself from the players as Duncan Fletcher had tended to before him.

Above all these, though, was Alastair Cook. Man of the Match twice, the clear choice for Man of the Series, and those 766 runs. Most good batsmen would die happy if they scored 766 Test runs in a whole career. Plenty never get the chance to do so. Cook did, at a young age, and now he was hitting the form of his life, form that would not waver for a good while yet. Importantly, his calm poise at the wicket helped bring through his teammates. Cook featured in many huge partnerships: there were seven stands worth 150 or more during the series, and all but one of them featuring Cook at one end.

Jonathan Agnew wrote a book on the series, *Aggers' Ashes*, and asked his fellow *Test Match Special* commentator, Jim Maxwell, to write its preface. Maxwell, whose exaggerated intonation laced with gravitas command immediate respect, has soaked up more hours of cricket than most on this planet and knows a good player when he sees one. He wrote: 'Alastair Cook's expedition was the most significant tour de force by a Cook since Captain James's visit in 1770, and his polishing skills made the kookaburra laugh at Australia's batsmen.'

The second part of this sentence was a neat reference to Cook's ball-shining skills. As noted after his Adelaide innings, Cook perspired significantly less than the average male athlete in hot and humid conditions. That meant he was almost the man to be tossed the ball in between deliveries. He could polish it on his cotton slacks, knowing it wouldn't get damp, and would have a good chance of staying as presentable as possible before tossing it back to Anderson or whichever other fast bowler was preparing to steam in at the Aussies.

In his afterword to his book, Agnew has this to say about Cook: 'Alastair Cook was an entirely transformed player, a complete revelation. I have seen him score all of his Test hundreds, and in none of them have I seen him bat anything like the way that he did in Australia. He became a completely different batsman, growing in confidence as the series went on. Cook has, like Anderson, a really steely centre and while he might give you a nice smile and friendly wave, he is actually a very driven and motivated individual. He had a horrible time against Pakistan and was an innings away from being dropped. To go on and bat as he did was remarkable and it says a lot for his self-effacing nature that he had really no idea, or apparent interest in, the records he had broken and the totality of his achievements.'

It was not, of course, purely sheer good fortune and a positive mindset that had elicited this dramatic renaissance in Cook's output. There was an important technical adjustment too. During the English season, he had lapsed into a bad habit, plonking his front foot down the line of off stump and then having to bring his bat down at a crooked angle to get to the ball. Now he was moving his feet more fluidly. One classic piece of advice for young batsmen from the coaching books is to lead with the head rather than any other part of the body. If a batsman moves his head first then the feet and everything else fall into line. Try it yourself. Stand up and imagine you are facing a bowler. Find a kitchen implement with a handle if you like. Now pick up your 'bat' and as the 'ball' starts coming towards you, move your head forwards to meet it. Natural gravity means your foot then comes down to where it needs to be for you to swing the bat through the appropriate angle. By contrast, Cook had adopted robotic trigger movements that obstructed his natural ability prior to the Australia tour. Now they were, thankfully, abandoned and he could go out and conquer, as Agnew correctly predicted.

'I suspect Alastair Cook is going to score more runs than anybody for English cricket – not only because he opens the batting, but also because of his age and the time he has ahead of him in his career. If he is not top of the tree by the time he finishes I will be absolutely staggered. He has an evident determination to carry on where he has left off in Australia, and will probably be Strauss's successor as captain. We don't know yet whether that will have an impact on the way he bats, but I would hope not.'

Agnew's advice to Cook, as laid out in his book, was to have somebody compile a before-and-after video with visual evidence showing everything he had done wrong in the home series against Pakistan compared with how he had just shown he could bat in Australia. It could be used, he suggested, in future times of uncertainty, to remind himself of what he unearthed, from a technical perspective, in the Ashes.

THE ONE-DAY CAPTAINCY

THE ONE-DAY CAPTAINCY

Alastair Cook was not required for the 2011 World Cup, but after England were thrashed in the quarter-finals by Sri Lanka, changes were sure to follow. England were still boarding the plane back from Colombo when the media started predicting the imminent resignation of Strauss from the captaincy. At the age of thirty-four, he would thus be given a bit more time off to spend with him family and to focus exclusively on Test cricket, where clearly there was no question whatsoever about his position.

The trouble was this: there was no obvious one-day captain to replace Strauss. David Hopps, writing in *The Guardian*, noted: 'England's problem is not so much that Strauss might stand down as the succession. With Paul Collingwood, the Twenty20 captain, also reaching the end of his international career, and Kevin Pietersen an increasingly unpredictable quantity, there is no obvious candidate to double up as a one-day captain at 20- and 50-over level.'

It took until early May for the ECB to come up with a solution, and it immediately looked a slightly awkward compromise. A bit like a chef trying to impress his diners with a piece of venison cooked three different ways, England did something similar with the captaincy, splitting it up three ways while hoping that it might all come together in some sort of coherent way. The strengths of Strauss as Test captain were manifest so no problem there, but then we had Stuart Broad as Twenty20 captain (an unexpected choice), and Cook as ODI captain (arguably even odder because he had not been considered good enough to be part of the World Cup team). Broad had featured in the team that had won the ICC World Twenty20 in the West Indies the previous year so there was logic there, and given the constrained nature of the shortest format, captaincy skills per se are rendered less important in Twenty20.

It was the selection of Cook as one-day captain that seemed stranger. There seemed to be one glaring candidate in the shape of Pietersen, who had led the England side previously in twelve ODIs and averaged 52.28 when doing so. Shockingly, in the twenty-seven matches since losing the stripes he had not made a century and averaged a woeful 23.78. When Pietersen had been sacked as captain after his brief tenure in 2008–09, the roadblock that apparently stopping him from doing his job properly was the then coach Peter Moores. Now, with Moores long departed, it appeared to be a good time for Pietersen to get a second bite of the bittersweet fruit. The ECB thought otherwise, and as things would become clear in due course, this was because the animosity towards Pietersen extended rather further than Moores.

Blogging for the BBC about Cook's appointment to the one-day captaincy, I noted that 'Nothing is vital in 50-over cricket until the next World Cup comes along in Australia and New Zealand in 2015. Cook's job is to ensure that, about three years from now, he has a nucleus of players who know where they will bat and how many overs they are likely to have to bowl. He can only do that by making sure he has the necessary support from a management who, for too long, have not accorded one-day cricket the respect it deserves. Thankfully, the 2015 World Cup will not be preceded by a strength-sapping Ashes tour which left the players mentally and physically exhausted, as had also been the case in 2003 and 2007.

'Cook will also have to lead by example, forming a close bond with whoever he is called upon to open the batting with, and show that the increased range of shot-making he demonstrated during his outstanding Ashes series can lend itself to one-day internationals.'

England began the Cook one-day era with a home series to Sri Lanka which they won 3-2 in a decider at Lord's. Craig

Kieswetter, who had been a success in the Twenty20 side, was Cook's opening partner. Both enjoyed good series, Cook top-scoring with 298 overall and the only century from an England batsmen, Kieswetter contributing 204. Cook also scored at an excellent rate, just a tick under a run a ball. The same could not be said about Bell and Trott, however, and the balance of the England team was all wrong. Absolutely no team other than England at the time had three steady accumulators in the team. It was, by now, pretty much all about power hitting. While you could just about warrant having one batsman in the anchor role, two was definitely a stretch and three was plain dumb. It so happened that Cook, bringing into the series his Ashes form, happened to be scoring quickly at the moment, but he wouldn't always, and with him, Bell and Trott in the same side there were, at certain points, going to be obvious pressure points during England's innings. Pointedly, Alex Hales, who looked an outstanding candidate to come into the side and give some muscularity to the batting, was overlooked.

While Bell and Trott were not blessed with one-day batting skills, they were becoming very good Test players and England duly won the Test series against Sri Lanka. Once again Cook, who could do absolutely nothing wrong in what undoubtedly was the golden phase of his career, was the leading batsman with 390 runs from four innings and two centuries. Bell was dismissed just once in amassing 331 and Trott was not far away. Strauss, on the other hand, suffered a hugely disappointing first series in his post-captaincy career, with a disastrous return of twenty-seven runs from four innings. There was plenty of time left for the Middlesex veteran to turn things around with four more home Tests against India to follow, but Cook was continuing to set new standards for himself, and his exploits were being eagerly lapped up. He had not turned into a household name; frankly, outside the global mass-market of football, it was getting harder and harder for an individual in a team sport to generate instant national recognition in Britain any more. However, Cook was now the benchmark that youth-level coaches used to explain the classical art of batting to prospective young players. Most youngsters would find Pietersen more exciting to watch, but many of his strokes were not in the coaching manual and attempts to emulate him tended to backfire. Cook was much more in the mould of Wally Hammond, Denis Compton, Colin Cowdrey, Geoffrey Boycott, Graham Gooch and Graham Thorpe. Pretty much every generation had seen at least one of these players at their best and were taught to hone their own technique and decision-making in such a way that it mirrored one of these players, rather than the more naturally expressive strokemakers such as Ted Dexter, Ian Botham or David Gower. In the current England team, Joe Root would be the coach's darling, less so Jos Buttler.

Cook's individual scores in the Tests against Sri Lanka were 133, 96, 106 and 55. The Sri Lankan attack was a good deal less menacing than it had been in past seasons. There was no Muttiah Muralitharan or Chaminda Vaas, for instance. Just because it looks like you should score runs does not mean runs come easily, though, as Strauss proved. Ever the perfectionist, Cook felt he could still improve in the Test arena by scoring runs more quickly if that was what the situation required. There was plenty of bad weather during that series, which finished 1-0 to England. Pushing for an unlikely win in the second match at Lord's, England needed quick runs in the second innings to give their bowlers something to work with afterwards. However, Cook managed just twenty-six in the morning session on the final day. He said afterwards: 'The team scored 111 runs in the two hours which was roughly what we were looking for. But I was late to react to the need to score quickly and I must learn from that.'

He also opened up a little further to explain how he had unlocked such a rich vein of form. 'There's no secret to it. Form comes and goes but it has stuck with me for a long time. A lot of it is hard work. I scored that double hundred in Brisbane and then backed it up with a century in Adelaide a week later. That gave me a lot of confidence – topping my confidence from 95 per cent to close to 100 per cent. That's a big difference. I went back to my old technique and worked with our sports psychologist, Mark Bawden, at the same time. Everything clicked.'

So much about what makes a sportsperson maintain maximum potential over a period of time depends on a number of variables. Innate ability, fitness, a positive attitude and a sprinkling of luck are among them – but having a clear, uncluttered mindset and one that knocks self-doubt into the long grass is one of the most pertinent. It is also the hardest factor of all to measure, but a cricketer frequently faces the same mental pressure as a golfer standing over a twelve-foot putt or a tennis player having to hit a second serve on match point up for a big win against a higher-ranked opponent.

Cook's body language very rarely betrayed any semblance of nerves at any point in his career, though he would not be human if he did not require some help at certain intervals in this area, and the fact he had sought out the help of the team psychologist – and that he had disseminated Mark Bawden's advice and made it work in his favour – suggested two things. Firstly, it gave the impression that the arrogance and stubbornness that he himself feels lurks within him was not such a big thing that it got in the way of that eternal hunt for excellence and improvement. Secondly, it showed that Cook was, by and large, able to use all the threads of advice that came his way, find the most useful elements within them, and turn them into a meaningful, positive end-product. This can have been no easy task. The England back-room staff was steadily growing to encompass any number of specialist coaches, analysts, advisers and so on. In some of the tour photos you can see a whole team of support staff alongside the playing staff. For a player to get any benefit from them as a collective unit it was probably sensible to listen to them in small doses. Cook was good at this, as his old cricket master at Bedford, Jeremy Farrell, noted.

India were expected to provide a much sterner Test than Sri Lanka. For one thing, they had won the series on their previous tour of England. For another, they had spent the previous year and a half ranked as the world number-one team in Test cricket. Then there were the personnel. Those three batting heavyweights – Sachin Tendulkar, Rahul Dravid and V.V.S. Laxman – were beginning to get a little long in the tooth but were still highly formidable opponents. The seam bowling department, an area of high focus internally since the retirement of Javagal Srinath, had in the meantime improved immeasurably.

As well as Zaheer Khan, the architect of India's 2007 series win when he was both leading wicket-taker and player of the series, they had Praveen Kumar and Ishant Sharma too, both accomplished bowlers who were a little faster than the typical Indian seamer and neither afraid to dish out a few verbals, throw in the odd bouncer, and generally aggravate batsmen as much as possible. This was expected to be a high-quality, spicy encounter. In the final analysis, it turned into a quite extraordinarily one-sided contest. England won the first Test by 196 runs, the second by 319 runs, the third by an innings and 242 runs, and in the fourth they must have taken their foot off the pedal because they only won it by an innings and eight runs. India were swept aside, treated with utter contempt by England who found the whole experience almost embarrassingly easy. M.S. Dhoni led the side and it should be stated that he had his work cut out when Zaheer picked up an injury early in the first Test, one he failed to recover from. Even allowing for that, one would have expected them to show more resolve. Even when the spinners came into the contest in the final match at the Oval, England bossed that department too. India's leg-spinner Amit Mishra took 0-170. Graeme Swann took 9-210.

Amid all this, Cook had an unusual series with scores of 12, 1, 2, 5 (yikes) and then 294 (!), and finally 34. The four low scores were largely irrelevant. Cook had banked so much credit that he would have now needed to go through a year or more of poor form before anyone could start questioning his position again. Clearly, that insatiable desire for huge runs was as intense as it ever had been, because the first time he even began to get going he produced one of Test cricket's great marathon efforts, one that almost deserves a chapter in its own right.

The match situation was as follows: already 2-0 down in the four-match series, India were bundled out for just 224 on the first day after Strauss had put them in first. Broad and Bresnan shared eight wickets, Anderson got the other two and Swann barely had time to turn his arm over. The innings came to an end when Cook completed one of his best catches in England whites, arguably his best of all. Anderson tried to tempt Ishant with a ball in the channel outside off stump which he hoped the tail-end batsman might nick to slip. Instead, he actually played a very good shot –

off the back foot, he punched the ball powerfully and pretty much middled it. Cook was the fielder positioned in the line of the ball, but at a dangerously close-in position, just in front of square on the off-side. Normally, the reaction when you are this close to a batsman playing an attacking shot is to duck out of the way. Cook didn't do that. He stood his ground and instinctively clutched at the ball as he turned his body. It was still 1,000-1 that he would grab it, however impressive his reactions were. Remarkably, the ball ended up snugly and, with a bit of good fortune, lodged in his armpit, and that meant the catch was good, however unorthodox it might have looked.

England marched off the outfield content with their performance on the day; Cook went to put his pads on and that catch must have helped him feel good about himself as he turned his attention to batting. He got going with one of those trademark punches off his hip that raced through the gap between mid-on and midwicket. This shot is the one that defines Cook the batsman, and I am convinced he finds it particularly easy because he is naturally right-handed rather than left-handed.

This may take some explaining, so here goes. Traditionally, a cricket coach would ask a child which hand he writes with and then tell him to hold the bat with his dominant hand at the bottom. That way a right-hand dominant player would bat right-handed, with his left leg facing the bowler, and so on. However, many excellent left-handed batsmen over the years have in fact been right-hand dominant. They include the modern big-hitting stars like Chris Gayle, Ben Stokes and David Warner, England's one-day captain Eoin Morgan, and plenty of big names from the past – Brian Lara, David Gower, Clive Lloyd, Michael Hussey, Matthew Hayden and Kumar Sangakkara. Oh, and Alastair Cook.

In addition, there are those who do it the other way – Sachin Tendulkar writes with his left hand and bats right-handed, alongside Michael Clarke, Inzamam-ul-Haq and Adam Voges. For decades, it had been speculated that it could not be down to pure chance that so many players batting the 'wrong way' were finding so much success. Then finally, in 2016, the science appeared to prove it.

Professor Peter Allen, from Anglia Ruskin University, noted that the first MCC coaching manual had instructed batsmen to pick up a bat in the same manner they would pick up an axe. This was not necessarily the right way to go about things, however, and after leading a study of 136 cricketers with a wide range of abilities, he drew this principal conclusion.

'While the MCC coaching manual advice might be beneficial for beginners, switching to a reversed stance gives elite players a technical and visual benefit,' noted the professor.

'We have limited our study to cricket, but the results may apply to other sports. In golf, three of the four men to have won a major playing left-handed were right-hand dominant, while other legendary golfers, such as Ben Hogan and Arnold Palmer, were left-hand dominant but played right-handed.

'In many cases, using a reversed stance has happened by chance. Golfer Phil Mickelson, a five-time major winner, is right-handed but learned to play left-handed to mirror his father's right-handed swing. Michael Hussey, one of Australia's finest cricketers, is right-hand dominant but learned to bat left-handed to emulate his childhood idol, Allan Border.

'In cricket, by adopting the conventional stance, batsmen may have been unintentionally taught to bat "back to front" and might not have maximised their full potential in the game.'

Dr David Mann, a scientist in human movement at VU University in Amsterdam, was able to explain more: 'The top hand is typically responsible for controlling and guiding the path of the bat to hit the ball, so it appears to be an advantage for the dominant hand to perform this role.'

In the particular case of Cook, he gave an interview in 2008 suggesting that the reason he was not able to hit sixes as easily as many of his contemporaries was because his stronger hand was at the top of the bat – thus, he could not get under the ball and muscle it over the heads of fielders as easily as others. However, on the flip side, by having his stronger hand on top he could benefit from having greater control. Turning back to where this all started – with that familiar punched shot off his hip scooting away for four – it is almost certain that the reason he finds it particularly easy to play that shot is that the dominant top hand is doing the work, riding the bounce, getting on top of the ball and then directing it where the gap is in the field.

Anyway, back to where we were. Thursday 11 August 2011 dawned with Andrew Strauss on fifty-two and Alastair Cook on twenty-seven. There were ninety overs of cricket in font of England's batsmen, who had all ten wickets in hand and were already just 140 runs behind India's score.

Cook's first four of the day was an assertive front-foot drive off Ishant Sharma, piercing the area between mid-off and extra-cover. He moved to forty-five with brilliant footwork off Sreesanth, stepping wide to meet a swinging half-volley and thumping it through cover. The same bowler switched to round the wicket, and Cook, his knowledge of the angles like a master snooker player, flicked him through square leg for four to reach a 130-ball half-century. It was fairly slow even by his standards, but the beauty was that the match situation did not demand any urgency. Looking for his first major contribution of the series, there would be no risks taken. Now he started feasting in his favoured area again, wide of mid-on, that dominant upper hand coming into play against spin and seam alike. Occasionally, the Indians would have to bowl a little wider of off stump to try something else, but the cuts and cover-drives were ruthless now. He remained patient, taking 213 balls to get to three figures, at which point England had lost only the wicket of Strauss and were now ahead of India's score.

Midway through day two, and with England in a dominant position, Cook could have relaxed a little, perhaps considered a more expansive strategy, with his job essentially done. But there are few enough occasions in batting when everything is in situ to just keep going almost indefinitely, and Cook firmly viewed the latter option as the more favourable approach. He already had a double century in the bank; how about another? And once you get to two hundred, well … then there's three hundred.

There was a period when Ishant Sharma got a little bit of lift, oddly enough from a ball nearly eighty overs old, and a couple of Cook edges on another day may have either crashed on to the stumps or ended up being pocketed in the slips. This was not one of those days. An almost ferocious pull shot took him to 150, and England 368-2.

England's other batsmen were on form too. Eoin Morgan, a terrific white-ball cricketer, only played sixteen Tests, but this was one of his best innings and he added a century of his own as England reached stumps on day two on 456-3 and continued where they left off on day three.

There was something almost metronomic in Cook's sectional

scoring rates. For example, he took 110 deliveries to get from 150 to 200, and 107 to get from 200 to 250. 'He just keeps going, Alastair Cook. Nothing to stop him,' said Michael Holding on commentary for Sky Sports. 'Too short,' added Michael Atherton as a wretched delivery from Sreesanth was smashed away for another boundary. 'They bowled really well at Cook in the first two Test matches and the start of this innings. But he's just ground them down and they've rather forgotten.'

England reached 666-6, a score ominous only for India. There was still time left for Cook to get to his first triple-century, a rare bird indeed for an English batsman. Gooch had scored a famous one in 1990 at Lord's (also against India) and even followed it up with a century in the same match. Was it time for the pupil to follow his mentor on to a hallowed plane?

With defensive fields in place, Cook had to time the ball perfectly to pick up boundaries, but he still did from time to time. Finally, a big cover-drive from Sharma was hit imperfectly, and flew off a fat edge to a fielder positioned in an unusual spot, three-quarters of the way back to the third man fence. Suresh Raina, the man completing the catch, looked disgruntled. There was certainly nothing left for India to celebrate. Cook was finally gone for 294, a marathon of marathons encompassing just shy of 13 hours and 545 balls, but England were able to declare on 710-7, as certain of a victory as a horse in a two-runner race when the other runner falls at the first fence. When Gooch, at the end of his 333, left a yawning gap between bat and pad to be bowled driving Manoj Prabhakar, the bowler spat out a ball of saliva on to the ground instead of celebrating. It is often this way at the end of a famous innings. It is relevant to point out that Gooch, in making 333, faced 60 balls fewer than Cook had in getting to

294. He would have been given time by Strauss to get his 300, but no more.

As I wrote in an article published by Firstpost, the online news website, 'The hunger to simply bat and bat was a greater incentive than the desire to aim big and overtake the 333 made by Gooch. Whereas Cook had pounced on some hopelessly wayward bowling from India on Thursday to reach 182, on Friday his was a vigil of remorseless accumulation.

'The bowling was improved – there was a commendable lack of short stuff to pull and cut away – so Cook found boundaries at a premium. Instead, he relied on his number-one asset: the intense concentration that can bore a hole in the heart of many a bowler. He defended the good balls, left the wide ones, and ran any ones and twos on offer with perpetual enthusiasm.

'While a succession of teammates came and went, Cook just kept on plodding along in his own way. He had licence to play freely; instead, he took the Trappist monk approach. He had a choice of taking a Maserati or a Hyundai hatchback out of the garage; he went for the Hyundai.'

It remains in the top ten for the longest Test innings ever played, and is also the highest individual score in a Test at Edgbaston. A piece on Cricinfo noted: 'Even those who wished for something a touch more flamboyant can't help but marvel at Cook's powers of concentration and remorselessness.'

In *The Guardian*, David Hopps suggested it was an innings that set up a guaranteed future stream of income for Cook, should he choose to pursue it. The Edgbaston epic, wrote Hopps, was the sort 'that will make him the darling of the corporate motivational speaking circuit fifteen years from now. Is your company down at heel? Are your employees lacking the Bulldog spirit? Call for Alastair Cook and ask him to tell the story of Edgbaston 2011. Dispense with the arctic explorers telling how they drove themselves through snowdrifts in sub-zero temperatures; consider no more the decorated soldiers, the great Olympians, the endless progression of sports coaches. Why, even dare to give Kevin Keegan the brush off. Let Alastair Cook relate how he batted for so long at Edgbaston that no one could quite remember when he began.'

England reached the fabled number-one spot in the world rankings after completing their win at Edgbaston, and reinforced that position at the Oval where the series whitewash was achieved.

This was the culmination of a pretty special period in English cricket. In the space of fifteen months, the national team had won the World Twenty20, an Ashes series in Australia, and had put themselves on top of the pile in Test cricket. It hardly stirred the nation's sports fans, however. Cricket has become an almost marginalised activity, struggling like every sport does for a bit of oxygen as football steadily increases its grip on society year by year. I was pleased to see England fans get excited about Gareth Southgate's team and their journey to the semi-finals of the 2018 World Cup. It's just a shame so many of those supporters cannot open their eyes to other sports.

CHAPTER THIRTEEN

PIETERSEN, STRAUSS, AND THE TEST CAPTAINCY

England now had a five-month gap between Tests. Their next series, of three matches, was scheduled for January 2012 in the UAE, which has become the established home for Pakistan cricket. No Test cricket has been played in the country of Pakistan itself since the terrorist attack on the Sri Lanka side in March 2009 exposed a lackadaisical and cavalier approach to security.

It goes without saying that the five-month gap between Tests did not mean England had no cricket at all planned. Far from it. The home Tests had barely finished before a ten-match series (five at home and then five away) against India was scheduled. Cook's team won the home series 3-0 – there was a washout and a tie – but lost every single game in India, a difficult experience which was, as ever, analysed quite ferociously by the media.

Even though Cook had not yet assumed the Test captaincy, he was almost certain to acquire it at some point, so he needed to learn on the job, as much as possible, in one-day cricket. He did not start particularly well. Unfavourable comparisons were drawn between his reactive approach and that of his opposite number M.S. Dhoni. Whereas the Indian captain relished an unorthodox approach, putting fielders in strange positions, never maintaining the status quo, always making the England batsman pause for thought, Cook had a plan and largely stuck to it.

That was not all. Sam Sheringham, on his BBC blog, reckoned: 'Some of the blame for his players' poor body language and indiscipline must be laid at the captain's door.' Cook reflected: 'Our Test side is on a slightly different journey than this one-day side. We have got a lot of experience in that Test team. A lot of people know their games inside out. We've been in a lot of different situations. Our one-day side haven't been through that.

You need experiences like that to realise what we've got to work on, but I can't fault any of the desire or effort to win.'

Turning to his own leadership, he added: 'It has been a very interesting experience. You do grow as a captain. Experiences like this certainly will help – although it's hard to find that now. Hopefully, I'm nowhere near where I could be in a few years' time.'

So England rested up at home for a couple of months before starting their defence of the number-one Test ranking spot early in 2012. In all, sixteen Tests were scheduled for England in the calendar year with only September and October clear of five-day action. Pakistan were up first, and Pakistan were not a team flush with star names. That mattered not, as England were easily beaten in the opening Test in Dubai, a disappointment considering they had scheduled two warm-up matches which they had won, but perhaps they were not quite as ready for the step up in grade.

That theory looked plausible when the teams moved from Dubai to Abu Dhabi, because now England were competitive. Stuart Broad bowled brilliantly as Pakistan hit just 257 batting first on a typically blameless wicket and England picked up a seventy-run lead when Cook (ninety-four) and Trott (seventy-four) led the way with the bat. When Panesar, playing his first Test in two and a half years, took 6-62 in Pakistan's second innings, England needed 145 to win the match and it looked a straightforward target. It was not. They were bowled out for just seventy-two, with Strauss (thirty-two) and Matt Prior (eighteen) the only men reaching double figures. Abdur Rehman, who only played in twenty-two Tests, took 6-25 with his slow left-armers. England were bowled out in thirty-six overs and instead of heading back to Dubai with all the momentum and the series up for grabs in the finale, it was a dead rubber scenario, which Pakistan won for good measure.

In Cricinfo's player ratings for the series, Cook was marked just five out of ten, despite facing more balls than anyone else and hitting the highest score. George Dobell noted: 'He generally sold his wicket more cheaply than has been case in recent times.'

The ODIs brought another swing of the pendulum and Cook suddenly found what was needed to get a team to tick in Asia. He was Man of the Series as England won it 4-0, and he averaged 80.75 against his 26.50 in the Tests. Now what? It was hard to predict anything any more. As Andy Flower had noted, England sweeping the ODIs in the UAE after being schooled in the Tests was 'exactly the opposite of what most people would have expected.'

Back on the permanent tour bus, whose wheels never stop turning, England's next stopover was Sri Lanka. When England lost the first Test, and did so comfortably, it raised two serious concerns. Had they lost the capability to be competitive in Asia? And were they wilting under the expectation that came with being the number-one Test nation? It was around this time that Strauss made the famous comment about how his side 'preferred being hunters than hunted'. It can be exhilarating when you reach the summit of a mountain, but the only way to go is to stand still or go down, and England suddenly seemed determined to seek a lower altitude.

However, when the teams moved from Galle to Colombo's P Sara Oval, having clocked up four defeats from four Tests in 2012, Cook scored ninety-four and forty-nine not out and England won by eight wickets, thanks in no small part to Graeme Swann's ten wickets in the match. In a match in which slow bowling was always going to be crucial, England's off-spinner had outbowled Sri Lanka's Rangana Herath. It all meant England retained their hold on the number-one ranking. Talking afterwards about the drawn series, Strauss said England's batsmen had needed to adjust their techniques when facing spin because the decision review system, now standard in Test cricket, meant batsmen were more likely to be dismissed lbw. Pietersen was particularly good in Colombo, hitting 151 off just 165 in an audacious and yet unhurried manner. The burden of captaincy, and the immediate disappointment of losing it, were at the back of his mind. It's unlikely he was getting on well with his teammates at this stage. He never really did, and it wouldn't be long before this flared up into a major issue.

Barely six weeks later, England played a three-match Test series against West Indies on home soil which they won 2-0. That was only to be expected. South Africa followed, and this was a much harder assignment. Strauss's form had become a real concern leading up to the rubber against West Indies, but he scored two centuries against them, only to last just four balls in the first Test against South Africa at the Oval. Cricket really can be an infuriating game at times. Nevertheless, England scored 385 against Graeme Smith's men, which looked a solid effort and Cook's steady 115 was the highest score. It ended a run of ten Tests without a century for him and was an important show of strength from England's lynchpin, with the number-one ranking officially up for grabs. It was Cook's twentieth Test century – he joined Pietersen and Strauss on that mark – with the long-standing England record of twenty-two, shared by Wally Hammond, Colin Cowdrey and Geoffrey Boycott, now firmly in the crosshairs for both these men. Who would get there first and who would end up establishing the new long-term record? Strauss was already thirty-five so it was unlikely to be him. At twenty-seven Cook was four and a half years younger than Pietersen so could be chalked up as a bookies' favourite though, as circumstances were to dictate, Pietersen's career would be seriously curtailed.

Cook was leaving well and driving smoothly. He hit one back-foot punch off the excellent quick bowler Dale Steyn that scooted away for four and hooked the same bowler for six. He was doing all the things well that he tends to do well when on form, and even though he departed early on the second morning, even at that point – with the score 271-4 – a score in the order of 450 appeared to be on the cards. England collapsed from that point on and South Africa exerted maximum pressure, piling up a remarkable 637-2 – including Hashim Amla's magnus opus, a marathon masterclass of 311 – and England were unable to escape with a draw. It is certainly unusual to lose a Test when reaching a high point of 251-2 on the first day, but England had contrived to do exactly that. 'It was our goal for a number of years to get to the top of the rankings and when you get there, you want to stay there,' said Anderson after that difficult Test at the Oval. 'We know if we lose the series, we won't stay there. People expect you to play as the number-one team in the world and we didn't do that this week.'

A Pietersen century in Leeds allowed England to salvage a draw in the second Test, but any sense of equanimity in the dressing room was shattered when he dropped a bombshell explaining, albeit in somewhat cryptic language, that outside status in the national set-up had become so extreme that drastic action might be required.

'I can't give any assurances that the next Test won't be my last,' Pietersen said. 'I'd like to carry on but there are obstacles that need to be worked out. There are other points I'm trying to sort out in the dressing room. It would be a huge shame. I love playing Test cricket for England. For me, the saddest part about all this is that the spectators just love watching me play and I love playing for England.'

Unable to indulge in the Indian Premier League (IPL) as much as he would like because of his central contract, and restricted from spending time with his family because of England's demanding schedule, Pietersen felt his individual concerns had been neglected. He was no longer playing ODIs for England because he was keen to be rested for occasional matches. On that issue, he was simply told to play all of them or none of them.

'It's absolutely 100 per cent not about money,' he added. 'This is not a money issue. The politics is what I have to deal with personally. It's tough being me playing for England.'

As the teams headed to Lord's in what had become a decider for the number-one ranking, Strauss said: 'I hope the Kevin issue isn't going to be a distraction,' possibly more in hope than with any realistic level of expectation.

Writing in the *Wisden Cricketers' Almanack*, Lawrence Booth drew a stark comparison with the mood portrayed by the world's best athletes in the country competing in the Olympics. 'The dysfunctional England dressing room felt depressingly out of kilter,' he observed.

As the build-up to Lord's continued, it emerged that Pietersen had sent text messages to the South Africans for which he subsequently felt the need to apologise. Even with the apology lodged, he was banned from the hugely important match at Lord's as punishment for his undisciplined use of his Blackberry device.

A year and a half later, in his book *KP: The Autobiography*, Pietersen unlocked his side of this simmering sideshow of insinuation and ill-feeling that had begun with his oh-so-brief captaincy tenure. In it, he admitted using derogatory language about Strauss in those text messages and that he had raised suspicions in the minds of Strauss and Andy Flower about his close friendships with South African players. (This should hardly have been surprising since Pietersen is, of course, a native South African.)

However, he insisted the ECB had no right to interpret Pietersen's actions as any evidence of 'open rebellion' or that he would have been divulging important tactics. There was an instance Pietersen cites in which he claims Strauss walked past and ignored him while he chatted to a South African player soon after the Headingley Test.

George Dobell wrote on Cricinfo at this time: 'It is increasingly hard to envisage a happy ending in the story of Pietersen's England career. From a position where there was a possibility that the Lord's Test might be his last, he has clumsily painted himself into a corner whereby he might not even play that game. At a time when England, faced with a foe who may well be stronger than them, require the team to be united and focused, Pietersen's post-match venting was most unfortunate.

'Pietersen, for all his posturing, for all his inconsistencies and for all his poorly expressed frustration, has a point. England's international schedule is overly onerous and, despite requests to act on it for years, the ECB has continued to pile demands upon its players. Pietersen is poorly advised, demanding and hard to manage. But that's why the ECB has a team of staff and managers. Now is the time for them to earn their corn. In particular, Hugh Morris, the manager of England cricket and, as such, the man who signs off the schedule and negotiates central contracts.

'Pietersen might also point to a certain hypocrisy within the ECB. There is an inconsistency with the treatment shown towards Pietersen and some other players.'

The conclusion to draw is that Pietersen is a character who is hard to incorporate into a team environment – a needy, childlike, highly sensitive person who craves attention. The complex task of trying to accommodate someone like this was something Strauss and Flower maybe did not have the energy to deal with, and however good Pietersen was as a player, having to focus so much attention on him was felt to be detrimental. However, perhaps if a new Test skipper was appointed and felt inclined to wrap a friendly arm around Pietersen's shoulder, that might help...

A new Test captain is exactly what England got after the Lord's Test, which had assumed so much importance on many levels, was won by South Africa. Frustratingly for Strauss's men, they managed to sneak a slim lead on first innings but ran into Hashim Amla again, on the form of his life, and were asked to chase 346 to salvage a draw in the series and to maintain an increasingly tenuous hold on that number-one ranking.

After a top-order collapse – the batting predictably weakened through the absence of Pietersen – some brave stuff from the lower order suddenly gave England a squeak. Then Graeme Swann was run out and Vernon Philander took the last two wickets quickly. South Africa won the series 2-0 and were the new top-ranked Test team. Perhaps, to some extent, it was a relief for England to finally hand over the ceremonial mace. It had weighed heavily.

Strauss took another week and a bit to ponder things before resigning. By the time he did, he had neatly led England in half of his hundred Tests and deflected attention away from the Pietersen situation and on to his poor form with the bat over the previous year and a bit, form which had seen his career Test average almost dip below forty. He elected to play no further professional cricket.

Cook, aged twenty-seven and already the one-day captain, was, of course, the only realistic heir to Strauss and was appointed Test captain on the same day the Strauss resignation was announced, in a carefully managed PR exercise from the ECB.

'Obviously I've got huge boots to fill,' said Cook. 'It feels like I've spent all my England career walking out to bat with him.' His captaincy of the one-day team was certainly holding up; of the eleven ODIs of that English summer, England won eight and lost two with one no-result. However, the next chapter had been scripted. It was all about the Test captaincy and whether that would hinder or enhance his remarkable productivity with the bat in England whites. It began with a four-Test series in India, the same place it had all started.

CHAPTER FOURTEEN

SUCCESS IN INDIA

W hen England won the Test series in India in 1984–85, they did it without Ian Botham or Graham Gooch. The bowling attack included the thirty-eight-year-old spinner Pat Pocock, and fringe players like Neil Foster and Norman Cowans. To win with that team they also needed a ton of runs from Mike Gatting and Tim Robinson, which they got, and given that it was a strong India they faced – featuring big names like Kapil Dev, Azharuddin, Vengsarkar and Shastri – to come from behind and win 2-1 was a serious achievement.

That series success grew in significance over subsequent years, and then decades. Gooch's team were stuffed out of sight in 1992–93, beaten again in 2001–02 and then there was the 2005–06 series in which Cook had made his debut, which was regarded as a major success story for England, even though they only drew the series. The 2008–09 series was, of course, another India win.

There wasn't exactly a thunderous degree of optimism about how England might fare on this latest foray against India. There were huge doubts about whether the batsmen had enough application to deal with the challenge of facing high-quality spin bowling, hour after hour. Remember, earlier in the year they had lost four out of five Tests played in the UAE and Sri Lanka. On the up side, Pietersen had crucially been integrated back into the side by now, and England scheduled three warm-up matches to ensure they had maximum exposure to conditions.

India cleverly put on flat wickets for those warm-ups, however, and then prepared a strip for the series opener in Ahmedabad that looked sure to help the team batting first. It was a bona fide 'road' initially, and India won the toss, put up 521-8 declared, and bowled England out for 191. The follow-on was enforced and Cook, in his first innings as the new full-time Test captain, struck a masterful

176. It needed one other big score of that ilk to get England out of jail in the same way they had managed in Brisbane two years earlier. Pietersen could not supply it. Nor could Trott, Bell or Nick Compton, Cook's new partner in lieu of Strauss. Eventually, some solid support came down the order from Matt Prior, but it was too late to prevent a nine-wicket win for India.

This latest Cook masterpiece may have come in defeat, but that is an irrelevance. It underlined his exceptional ability to recognise what was within his scope of influence and execute his response to perfection. On a typical fourth-day wicket in India, the ball comes on to the bat slower than previously and the bounce is low and somewhat variable. Cook tended to attack the short ball in this innings, appreciating the risks associated with driving. He cut and pulled the spinners, and worked the fast bowlers square of the wicket.

Gooch called it the best innings he had seen his protégé produce up to that point, and went further, saying Cook was now 'one of the best players in the world.'

By scoring a big century when the wicket was beginning to help the bowlers, Cook had led by example in his first match as the permanent England Test captain. Now it was down to his teammates to replicate his actions.

The second Test was staged at Mumbai's Wankhede Stadium, where England had famously won under Andrew Flintoff's captaincy in the only Test that Cook had missed since he had started his England career. Mumbai, India's most modern city, often attracts a healthy contingent of England supporters, and in late November the humidity is not as bad as it can be at other times of the year. Once again, England lost the toss but they did not despair. First of all, they judged the pitch accurately by picking two specialist spinners – bringing in Monty Panesar, in place of Tim Bresnan, to support Graeme Swann and the part-time slow bowler Samit Patel. Cook would have had a major influence in this decision. Panesar rewarded the faith shown in him by Cook and Andy Flower by removing Virender Sehwag for thirty and Sachin Tendulkar for just eight, and even though Cheteshwar Pujara's 135 ensured India banked a 300-plus score they were restricted to 327, as Panesar and Swann shared nine wickets in all.

In response, Cook and Compton put on sixty-six for the first wicket before Pragyan Ojha snared both Compton and then a horribly out-of-form Trott for a duck. Cook and Pietersen – whatever they felt about each other off the pitch – gelled gloriously well, as they often had in the past, to put on 206 together. Both hit centuries, Pietersen going big with 186 and England established a healthy lead of 86. When Cook and Pietersen are in partnership together it is particularly hard for bowlers to counter them. They are different in just about every respect. One is right-handed, naturally aggressive, unpredictable and often hits premeditated shots; the other is left-handed, methodical and generally cautious. Whereas Cook will be happy to defend for an hour if required and then put away three bad balls in succession, Pietersen needs a 'release' shot every so often to feel happier about himself. It is sometimes possible, as a bowler, to build up pressure on Pietersen and buy his wicket that way. It is almost impossible to do the same thing to Cook.

By the time England's first innings had come to an end, there remained an awful lot of work for the touring side to accomplish. After seeing England's spinners take nine wickets in the first innings, Cook allowed Panesar to share the new ball with Anderson. It was an inspired move. In his fourth over, Panesar had Sehwag caught off a thick defensive edge and now Cook put Swann on at the other end. Extraordinary to relate, it was the only bowling change he had to make in the innings. Swann and Panesar, the latter taking eleven wickets in the match, ran through the Indian line-up. There were lovely little bonuses, like Virat Kohli hitting a horrible Swann full toss straight to mid-off and Ravichandran Ashwin trying something outlandish before he had even begun to assess conditions.

Cook had the luxury of going out to bat again with just fifty-seven runs wanted for a memorable win and, together with Compton, he made sure of a thumping ten-wicket win. India one: England one. Two Tests to go. Game on. Game very much on.

India were now in something of a quandary. Should they instruct the groundsman for the third Test in Kolkata to ensure a result, with spin and bounce in the wicket? If so, then it would have the same ingredients in it that allowed Swann and Panesar to be so effective in Mumbai, where the England spinners had been much more successful than India's. The eighty-three-year-old curator at Eden Gardens, Prabir Mukherjee, also found himself in the spotlight as he refused to produce a wicket that would turn prodigiously from the word go. In truth, such a tactic would have been a wild gamble.

As so often in Test cricket, one team was deemed by the media to be carrying momentum into the match, and that team was England. Yet again, India won the toss and this time were bowled out for 316 against a very disciplined England attack, with Panesar in his absolute element now, taking 4-90 from 40 overs – drying up runs and taking wickets at the same time.

England needed to try to repeat what they had done in Mumbai now – bat patiently and bat big, building as big a lead as possible. The wicket had turned out to be fairly flat by all accounts but, as is so often the case in India, runs needed to be squeezed out of the surface – you couldn't stand tall and tap it into a gap for four like you could in Australia.

Cook was now in absolute peak form. I'd argue that he was batting better than he did even on the Ashes tour in 2010–11, given that his runs there came against an ill-disciplined attack and with a ball that came on to the bat more readily. Alastair Cook, the new captain of England, only knew how to score centuries all of a sudden. After 176 in Ahmedabad and 122 in Mumbai came an innings that trumped both of these knocks: 190 in Kolkata. He batted for two and a half sessions on the second day and a session and a half on the third day, hitting twenty-three fours and two sixes off 377 balls. Most significantly of all, he scored his runs more quickly than every Indian batsman bar Sehwag and Yuvraj Singh, and while some of this was down to the fact that one of India's spinners, Ashwin, was badly out of sorts, he had also partially been knocked out of his comfort zone by the exploits of Cook and Pietersen in the first two innings.

The *Daily Telegraph* list that rates Cook's best Test innings has occasionally been referred to previously in this book. It places this particular innings top of the charts and it is very hard to argue against that. Rob Bagchi reasoned: 'His fifth hundred in five Tests as captain, and third during [spoiler alert] the first away-series victory over India for twenty-seven years illustrated Cook's mastery during his golden honeymoon since succeeding Strauss full-time, sweeping India's spinners to distraction and, like a seemingly staid old man suddenly revealing that his name was Gene Kelly, surprising everyone with the twinkling use of his feet to smash them for straight sixes.'

To produce five hundreds in five Tests as captain – remember the two in which he had been stand-in captain? – was a phenomenal achievement in its own right. This fifth one, when he still had not fully wedded himself to the captaincy job and in the midst of a fiercely competitive series, was a humdinger, no doubt about it.

Cook felt his ability to score at faster than three runs an over during his 190, when scarcely anyone else managed the feat, was attributable to the extra aggression he felt compelled to find in order to continue to merit his spot in the one-day side. He joined Everton Weekes, Garry Sobers, Ken Barrington and, neatly, Andy Flower to be the third visiting batsman to hit three successive centuries in Tests. Having equalled the England record of twenty-two centuries in Mumbai, he had set a new one just eleven days later. He went past seven thousand runs in eighty-six Tests, getting there faster than legendary players of the game like Viv Richards, Ricky Ponting, and Greg Chappell – and he was the first person to get there before reaching their twenty-eighth birthday.

He did give one chance, a low edge to first slip on seventeen. That was a very expensive miss by Cheteshwar Pujara. Even when Cook was finally out, the dismissal happened in bizarre circumstances – a run-out achieved by Kohli, who threw down the stumps at the non-striker's end from the infield. Cook, his brain momentarily malfunctioning (and how rare was that?), had ample time to drop his bat behind the crease. However, he did not do so, as he half flinched away from the flight of the ball. There is a provision in the game's laws for a batsman to avoid dismissal in such circumstances, should it be deemed he is taking evasive action. The umpires did not feel that was the case and Cook certainly did not believe he had a right to be exonerated.

Cook was helped by a real team effort in the batting as Compton, Trott and Pietersen hit half-centuries before Prior, Swann and Samit Patel contributed further runs down the order. England got to 523, but there remained a chance India might get something out of the game. That notion was dispelled when England's bowlers got to work on the fourth day and it took a gutsy ninety-one from Ashwin to avoid a heavy innings defeat. England had to knock off just forty-three to secure a 2-1 series lead, made a bit of a mess of it in truth when losing three wickets, before Bell stroked four boundaries, and that was that.

Even for someone as consistently modest as Cook always was about his achievements, his comments afterwards almost pushed the envelope to absurd degrees. 'I've been hitting the ball all right on this tour,' he said. 'It's nice to contribute to the team's success. To score runs here you've got to bat a long period of time. I had a bit of luck on and I managed to cash in.' Cook's Test average was now in excess of fifty. He could not sustain it. The high point had been reached, but what a zenith it was, all the same, for a one-time chorister from a sleepy town in Essex.

At Nagpur, England needed to come away with a win or a draw to join the 1984–85 tourists and carve out a little place in history with a series win in India.

In terms of pitch preparation, India had run out of ideas because whether a wicket turned moderately (Kolkata) or quite a bit (Mumbai), England – rather than the home side – had found all the right answers. It was the first time since 1999 –2000 that India had lost two home Tests in a row and they really wanted to salvage the series, so a drawn match would be no good. So even though ideas may have been thin on the ground, a flat pitch would be pointless and a dry one was prepared for Nagpur.

Yuvraj Singh was dropped; Sachin Tendulkar could not be dropped, such was his status, but he was struggling for runs. Most of the bowlers had disappointed, notably the off-spinner Ashwin, who was fairly new to the Test set-up but had done well in ODIs.

For once, England won the toss, but both openers were dismissed in the first hour. India still refused to acknowledge the benefits of the decision review system at this time. Had it been in place, Cook would certainly have avoided a poor lbw decision against him. It was tough going for all the batsmen, even Pietersen, whose 73 occupied 188 balls. Joe Root was ushered in to make a surprise debut and did well, also scoring 73. Cook must take much of the credit for this. With the out-of-form Samit Patel dropped, a more conservative approach would have been to bring in either Jonny Bairstow or Eoin Morgan, both of whom had Test experience. The shared opinion of Cook, and Flower was to go with Root instead and the young Yorkshireman had been identified as a strong player of spin.

The pitch had turned out to be ultra- low and ultra-slow, and would be a serious test of a batsman's patience throughout. For the team that didn't need to win – England – that meant it was paramount not to provide presents for the bowlers, and they stuck manfully to the task, losing just five wickets on the first day and batting for 146 overs in all in their first innings.

The match reached day four before India declared their first innings on 326-9, still four runs behind England, Dhoni having grown impatient watching the tail-enders poke and eager to have another go with the ball. Cook made just thirteen before he was then unfairly triggered by the same umpire, Dharmasena, who had wrongly given him out in the first innings, but there were few alarms from then on for England. Trott and Bell hit centuries, the Test was drawn, and the series was won.

Cook joined Douglas Jardine, Tony Greig and David Gower as only the fourth England captain to win a Test series in India. He reflected afterwards: 'It is obviously a very special day, a special tour,' he said. 'I think it is on a par with the Ashes. As an Englishman winning in Australia after so long meant a huge amount. But to be in that dressing room there for that last half an hour knowing what we had achieved was a very special place and it will live long in my memory.

'Everyone in this squad can be proud of what they achieved, especially the way we bounced back after the heavy defeat in Ahmedabad. I was surprised at the level we managed to achieve so soon after Ahmedabad, to put all those doubts to bed and prove to ourselves that we could bat in these conditions. After the first game in Ahmedabad it would have been so easy to let heads drop, but we showed a lot of character in Mumbai.

'The fact it was a result wicket in Mumbai really helped us. It freed us up knowing that one way or another there would be a result and that people weren't expecting us to win. Once we got over that mental hurdle and were able to trust our ability on these wickets with the bat, we certainly made a big leap forward.'

Cook also addressed his personal milestone of scoring a century at the first time of asking, albeit in a losing cause.

'You want to prove that the captaincy is not a burden. To do it straight away is a big monkey off your back. It made me very proud that night when I went home after the game. If it gave other people confidence, that is even more pleasing. They are big characters in the dressing room. The support they have given me … I couldn't have asked for anything more. To captain those guys can be tough in certain circumstances, but you want that, you want a lot of ideas and strong opinions because that is when you normally get the best thinking done.'

CHAPTER FIFTEEN

CHAMPIONS TROPHY AGONY

In March 2013, England played three Tests in New Zealand and neither team managed to win a game. There was a fair bit of rain, particularly in the second match in Wellington which England dominated, but they were in deep trouble in the final match at Auckland. That was until a final-day rearguard masterminded by Ian Bell and Matt Prior, and then Stuart Broad, of all people – who hit six runs in two and a quarter hours – left the Black Caps cursing. England had clung on, with one wicket remaining.

A couple of months later, England returned the favour by hosting New Zealand for a short two-Test series, and both those matches were won by Cook's men. The skipper contributed yet another century, his fifth since assuming the captaincy, in the second Test at Leeds. Questions were asked, however, about his reluctance to enforce the follow-on in that match. The loss of the opening day to rain combined with further bad weather forecast for the final day left a limited window to finish off the match. England were really beyond safe when Cook finally declared at 287-5, deep into the fourth day, leaving New Zealand a notional target of 468.

With only forty-five minutes of play possible before lunch on the final day and no further cricket until 3pm things got a little bit tight, but Cook's tactics, however cautious they may have appeared, had paid off. He spikily defended his strategy, saying: 'The result definitely vindicates the decision. There is absolutely no doubt about that at all. To win by 250 runs is a good win and in just over three days' cricket, effectively, it is an outstanding performance. You are judged as a captain on results. In this game we have won by 250 runs. I woke up this morning and the first thing I did was look out the window. We knew rain was about, but we thought there would be a few windows of opportunity.'

This was the first time Cook's strategical approach to Test captaincy had been questioned. It would certainly not be the last, but the next immediate concern was the Champions Trophy, a short multi-team tournament run by the ICC as a sort of mini World Cup, but a prestigious contest all the same. England had been beaten in one final on home soil in 2004. Cook had the chance to remedy that.

England beat Australia, lost to Sri Lanka and then had to beat New Zealand in Cardiff in a match reduced to twenty-four overs per side to make the semi-finals. Cook top-scored with a breezy 64 from 47 balls in a total of 169 and England got home by ten runs. He hit two sixes in an international innings for the first time, both hit cleanly down the ground, and even showed his ability to play some of the trendy new shots he would never had learned under Derek Randall at Bedford. There was, for instance, a paddled scoop for four in this innings. He was averaging a creditable 44.79 in ODIs since taking on the captaincy, having managed just 30.52 beforehand.

England thrashed South Africa in the semi-final and found themselves in a final against India. Surely this was the moment to end so much heartache in 50-over tournaments. Fans of a certain age could remember a number of near misses.

England reached three of the first five finals of the Cricket World Cup, between 1979 and 1992, without winning any of them. They lost by seven runs to the Aussies in Kolkata in 1987, and by twenty-two runs to Pakistan in Melbourne five years later. Though all the World Cups since then have featured desperately poor English performances, in the 2004 Champions Trophy final at the Oval they were in total command against West Indies before failing to finish the job off.

Nine years on, India were the opponents at Edgbaston and the weather turned the final into a twenty-overs-per-side affair. England's batting unit – with Cook, Bell and Trott occupying the top three positions – was not well suited to Twenty20 at all, so they had to bowl well to have a sniff. They did exactly that, holding the Indians to 129-7, but the chase was going nowhere until Ravi Bopara and Eoin Morgan got to work. Both batted well and were set to reel in the target quite comfortably, but then it all went horribly wrong. They departed to consecutive deliveries in the eighteenth over – poor balls, frankly, bowled by Ishant Sharma that were not quite middle and were instead gobbled up by Ashwin catching on the leg side. That left England needing twenty from fourteen balls with four wickets in hand. They still should have won it, but continued to lose their way and fell six runs short. It was very frustrating to watch it all unfold because England had played better cricket than India for the bulk of the match.

Cook should have been lifting the trophy. He didn't get to do that. He continued to captain the England one-day team until just before Christmas the following year when he was sacked after the team had run up five consecutive series losses under his leadership. Morgan would take over the team for the 2015 World Cup, a tournament Cook never got to play in. Even then, the management failed to select the right type of batsmen until things changed quite radically in the summer of 2015, and the consequences were immediately positive – dynamic, explosive batting and some extremely encouraging results.

The Ashes followed on from the Champions Trophy, and this time the two old enemies would face each other for ten consecutive Tests – the first five in England, the next five in Australia. They would be really sick of the sight of each other by the end of that.

Australia, under the captaincy of Michael Clarke, were by now a pale shadow of the team they had been for so long, and England were warm favourites, at least for the five-match home rubber. The series was won 3-0, a satisfactory result for sure on paper, though there were niggling issues.

The opening match at Trent Bridge was a weird head-scratcher of a game, with Australia's final pairing putting on 163 in the first innings to convert a total of 117-9 into 280, and then 65 in the second innings, to almost rescue a win from a wholly unconvincing position.

Cook relied heavily on the skills of Anderson in that Trent Bridge Test. Jimmy was his great friend and had been, by some distance, the most consistently skilful fast bowler in the side during their shared careers. While Stuart Broad had the ability to produce killer spells to win games, Anderson was the technician who kept chiselling away at the opposition, constantly honing and adapting his own craft to keep ahead of the competition.

One of the key themes of Cook's Test captaincy was that he continued to get the very best out of Anderson. Fast bowlers do have limited energy reserves, though, and need a break from time to time. At Trent Bridge, after Anderson's three key strikes on the final morning left England a wicket away from victory, Cook finally rested Anderson after a thirteen-over spell and Australia immediately prospered with Brad Haddin and James Pattinson at the crease.

Cook showed he could resort to cynical time-wasting – in the run-up to lunch, he and Broad engineered a situation that required the bowler to have his boots repaired and then changed altogether. Cook was desperate to use the lunch break to give Anderson further rest so he could then toss him the ball immediately after the break. That tactic worked and England won by fourteen runs.

If Cook had not yet developed a reputation as a cautious captain, he certainly had done by the end of the Trent Bridge Test. That final day had started with Australia wanting 124 runs with four wickets in hand. Cook posted a single slip in place to the seamers, while Graeme Swann bowled with long-off and long-on in place. Accordingly, Australia scored slowly. Fortunately, when they did edge the ball, which they did three times, it went to the solitary slip (Cook himself, as it happened). It also demonstrated that if he did not quite trust a bowler in a sticky situation, he would not give him the ball. Steven Finn bowled twenty-five overs in the match, compared to Anderson's fifty-six. Cook's captaincy on that final day was applauded by Andy Flower, who told the press: 'He led them well. He showed his strength and calmness as a captain again.'

Things were a whole lot more straightforward at Lord's, with England winning by 347 runs, no less, and Cook able to reduce Anderson's workload quite significantly – but they were dicey at Old Trafford where Australia had the upper hand when the weather intervened.

England's batsmen under-clubbed at Chester-le-Street but Stuart Broad was sensational in both innings with the ball to seal the series verdict with a match to play. At the Oval, the honours were shared.

The trip to Australia that followed was a chance for England to win a fourth Ashes series in succession and start pushing hard once again for that number-one ranking. There were reservations – England had been slightly flattered by that 3-0 scoreline and on their home territory it was reasonable to expect the Aussies to be a more formidable beast.

What nobody could have expected was the crushing ignominy of a 5-0 defeat which ripped the guts out of the team, ended careers, and triggered some extended soul-searching. The whole fabric of the England team was torn down and had to be rebuilt. Cook, Anderson and Broad simply never engaged first gear. They were beaten by enormous margins – 381 runs, 218 runs, 150 runs, 8 wickets and finally 281 runs.

There were major problems off the pitch to deal with too. After the Brisbane Test, Jonathan Trott pulled out of the tour with severe anxiety and stress issues, and barely played for England again. Graeme Swann, with unexpected suddenness, lost his confidence completely amid some niggling fitness concerns, and retired from cricket as the players assembled in Melbourne at Christmas just before the fourth Test.

These would prove two huge obstacles to overcome in due course. Swann was not only England's but the world's leading Test wicket-taker in the five years since he had made his debut, while Trott's sheer dependability had enabled to him to deliver a barrage of runs, principally in the winters of 2010–11 and 2012–13.

Flower, too, decided enough was enough after the Australian tour, one that also included heavy defeats in ODI and the Twenty20 series, and soon after that one of the most extraordinary episodes of English cricket unfolded. It began with a blandly worded statement from the England and Wales Cricket Board with a shocking top-line message – essentially, the senior management team at the ECB had decided to end the international career of Kevin Pietersen indefinitely and forthwith. This was a wholly unprecedented type of announcement altogether.

Imagine a player being so thoroughly marginalised by the very people whose job it is to integrate the most talented cricketers in the land ... that those same people would unilaterally rule that one of those cricketers would never play for his country again in any format.

Pietersen was certainly a very difficult individual to deal with, but not all teammates are friends. Many of the best teams in professional sport are almost certainly peopled by problematic, selfish, needy individuals with whom the guy sitting next to them in the dressing room might not choose to split a few beers the same evening.

Individuals who were not in the dressing room, administrators like Giles Clarke and Paul Downton, had pretty much decided enough was enough with Pietersen. While other players, by and large, took the central contract on offer and made themselves available to play, Pietersen did things differently. In their ECB offices, Clarke and Downton had grown irritated by Pietersen's various demands. They also had a series of black marks by his name, having noted his role in the downfall of Peter Moores – who ironically would be chosen as the man to replace Flower – and how he had tested Andrew Strauss's patience and lost the former captain's trust.

Cook's role in the saga was initially unclear, even though he was obviously involved in the discussions that led to the nuclear option being selected – namely this frankly bizarre permanent severance arrangement in which Pietersen, it appeared, would not and could not be considered for selection ever again. In the final analysis, Cook would be shown to be almost a neutral bystander. While he was not particularly sympathetic to the plight of Pietersen, any suggestion that he was secretly cooking up plans with Giles and Downton to cut the mercurial South African adrift was grossly off target. Perhaps the team captain should have taken a stronger stand, one side or the other. Perhaps the issue was so complex that he simply found it too hard to do so. Either way, it was ludicrous for ECB detractors and Pietersen fan-club leaders like Piers Morgan to pin the blame on Cook. The former tabloid newspaper editor called the England captain a 'repulsive little weasel' on Twitter.

CHAPTER SIXTEEN

PERSONAL FRUSTRATIONS

On 4 February 2014, *The Guardian* ran an online poll asking its readers if the England and Wales Cricket Board was right to end the international career of Kevin Pietersen? A landslide result was revealed, with 73 per cent believing the governing body had got this big decision wrong.

Why the public love for Pietersen? He was arguably a declining force with the bat and had batted very poorly in Australia, though he was not alone in that regard. Certainly people remembered the good things he had done, his innings at the Oval in his first Test series that finally decided the epic struggle for the 2005 Ashes, his heavy scoring in the Caribbean that made him Player of the Tournament five years later when England won the ICC World Twenty20. To many lovers of the sport, these things weighed more heavily on hearts and minds than a few inappropriate tweets or texts here or there, or the odd scrap of off-the-record detail fed to the media.

There was one other major factor at play here. My suspicion is that he attracted great swathes of sympathy by being portrayed as an outcast, the ugly duckling in the team, the victim, the scapegoat. People simply abhorred the notion that Pietersen might have been deliberately left to stew in a fog of unhappiness towards the end of his England career, rather than given a helping hand to re-establish himself as a top-class player. Those suspicions were given added credence when Andrew Strauss was overheard calling Pietersen 'a complete c***' in an off-the-cuff remark a few months later during a commentary stint. (He thought he was off air, but users on the Fox Sports app in Australia heard the words loud and clear while Strauss commentated on an MCC v Rest of the World exhibition match.)

To establish a definitive timeline of events is not easy. What we *do* know is that on the same day *The Guardian* ran its poll assessing the public position on Pietersen, the ECB chose to provide no details whatsoever of any specific breaches of team discipline by the South African-born player. It did say that the members of the England management team were unanimous in electing to rebuild without him, and that the thirty-three-year-old's recent history of knee trouble was an aggravating factor.

Michael Vaughan made the point that whoever would come in as the new coach – Moores had not been re-appointed at this point – should have the ultimate call on what to do about Pietersen, while Nasser Hussain agreed with Vaughan's demand for greater clarity from the ECB, while also charting Pietersen's colourful track record of upsetting almost any institution or individual who had tried to manage him.

'However disruptive a player is, you can still try to manage most players,' Hussain told Sky viewers. 'But history tells you with Kevin, he hasn't really got a foot to stand on, whether it be back in Natal or Hampshire or Nottinghamshire, or Peter Moores or Andrew Strauss or Alastair Cook or Andy Flower – wherever he has been he has been a problem.

'Eventually English cricket has said "enough is enough". Some people believe in cutting out the virus and moving on; other people just say "man-manage your best players". There is no easy solution. He is arguably one of the best players England have ever produced. Andy Flower said they are going to have to take some pain, going into this new era, and I think we all know and see now what he meant by that.'

Soon afterwards, much more juicy details emerged in the press about what had been really going on behind the scenes in the dark final days of the Ashes tour.

Andy Flower had, it appeared, singled out Kevin Pietersen for blame as relations between Flower and the players broke down. Flower painted a picture of open rebellion in which Pietersen had attempted to trigger a players' revolt in Australia against the Zimbabwean's intense coaching style. Unlocking this secret sealed Flower's fate – he accepted his own resignation was inevitable, but because he cared deeply about the future of the elite game in England (and perhaps because he had other options lined up within the ECB set-up) he was determined to ensure Pietersen would play no part in any future England side. David Hopps, writing on Cricinfo, said Flower believed Pietersen 'posed a danger to team unity' but that this conviction 'was only partly justified by events and owed much to memories of how Pietersen had already brought down a previous England coach, Peter Moores, five years earlier.'

More and more people were growing disillusioned with the ECB's handling of the matter, rather than rallying around the establishment. The newly retired Graeme Swann said: 'I could have understood if Kevin's career with England had finished after "textgate". But to go through the reintegration process and then, just fifteen months later, discard him for good seems very strange. Clearly, Kevin must have upset people enough for the England hierarchy to decide he is no longer wanted. Don't forget, we're not talking about a middling player here – we're talking about a batsman of sublime talent. As I say, I saw nothing while I was on the Ashes tour. His approach was spot-on.'

It is almost certain during the Ashes that Pietersen was not the only player who had grown disenchanted by Flower's coaching methods, which had tended to suffocate the players' natural expression. Pietersen was the only player who was bold enough, or stupid enough, to bring it out into the open, however, when Cook and Prior held a clear-the-air team meeting without coaching staff present. This took place on what would have been the final day of the Melbourne Test, had England lasted that long in the match.

Adopting a tone of voice which shocked many players, Pietersen launched into an astonishing attack on Flower, but he received little support and many players soon felt guilty about the meeting as a result. Ultimately, they retained respect for Flower's integrity and determination to provide them with the best tools for success in the cut-throat world of elite cricket. Effectively, Flower himself ensured he retained the backing of the players when he asked to see them individually and for them to choose, ultimately, between his way or the Pietersen way.

Hopps concluded: 'Any imaginings Pietersen had that he could stoke a wider rebellion were proved to be illusory. His lack of empathy with the general mood, which tends to be consumed by his own ego, has previously been suggested as a tragic character trait that has repeatedly cost him.'

On 9 February, five days after its initial statement and with Twitter awash with rumours and squabbles featuring input from Matt Prior, Cook's vice-captain, and Tim Bresnan, both of whom were seeking to defend Cook's character and the status quo at large, the ECB provided further detail on the Pietersen sacking.

The statement, which was not attributed to any individual within the governing body, declared: 'The England team needs to rebuild after the whitewash in Australia. To do that we must invest in our captain Alastair Cook and we must support him in creating a culture in which we can be confident he will have the full support of all players, with everyone pulling in the same direction and able to trust each other. It is for those reasons that we have decided to move on without Kevin Pietersen.

'Following the announcement of that decision, allegations have been made, some from people outside cricket, which, as well as attacking the rationale of the ECB's decision-making, have questioned, without justification, the integrity of the England team director and some of England's players. Clearly what happens in the dressing room or team meetings should remain in that environment and not be distributed to people not connected with the team. This is a core principle of any sports team, and any such action would constitute a breach of trust and team ethics. While respecting that principle, it is important to stress that Andy Flower, Alastair Cook and Matt Prior, who have all been singled out for uninformed and unwarranted criticism, retain the total confidence and respect of all the other members of the Ashes party. These are men who care deeply about the fortunes of the England team and its image, and it is ironic that they were the people who led the reintegration of Kevin Pietersen into the England squad in 2012.'

The effect of this was simply to polarise public feelings one way or another. What people really resented was the 'people outside cricket' phrase, a horribly misjudged comment that regarded with disdain anyone not employed in a professional capacity in the sport. In other words, the very people who helped pay the staff wages at the ECB, through their Sky Sports subscriptions and the tickets they bought at the gate, were looked down upon as mere riff-raff. This attitude, frankly, stank to high heaven. The ECB has essentially ridden roughshod over the choked grass-roots of the game through its determination to claw in as much cash as it can from Sky, while simultaneously starving the free-to-air channels of any cricket content whatsoever that might draw the youngsters in. I can personally attest to a worrying lack of interest in cricket at youth level on the club scene in England and figures from Sport England show participation is falling.

However, in terms of where England would be going in the post-Pietersen era, the ECB, however ugly its reputation was becoming among the supporters, could at least prepare for the future with a clean slate. Crucially, none of the other centrally contracted players still involved after the Ashes had followed Pietersen out of the door, whether through choice or obligation.

Most salient of all was that Cook's personal reputation was largely unsullied. Nobody, other than the most blinkered folk, seriously believed that the poisonous remarks dished out by Piers Morgan were the result of any special information which he, of all people, was privy to.

In April, Peter Moores was somewhat curiously given a second bite of the cherry. Five years after being sacked as England coach he was given the job again and the main task at hand was hauling England back up the Test rankings so that they could challenge for the number-one spot and try to oversee a World Cup campaign that might be slightly less embarrassing than the previous five.

Only a few months into the new Moores regime, further light was shed on the axing of Pietersen and, more specifically, Cook's role in it. Pietersen's book, *KP: The Autobiography*, detailed its author's claims of a bullying culture in the dressing room, led by a clique of Graeme Swann, Stuart Broad and Prior, who was its leader, and with partial assistance from James Anderson. Pietersen said the bowlers had mocked bad fielding, and forced fielders who dropped catches off their bowling to apologise to them afterwards. Prior came in for the most forceful criticism as a 'massive negative influence', while Flower was 'contagiously sour, infectiously dour' and 'horrendous to work with'.

Interestingly, Cook, who was captain of a team that had Flower as its coach and Prior as its vice-captain, escaped with limited criticism from Pietersen. He does note that Cook looked down at his shoes during a five-minute meeting in which he told the player he was no longer required to play for his country. 'I feel sorry for him, it must be one of the most uncomfortable experiences of his career,' wrote Pietersen. He also adds that 'while Cooky is a nice man, he is also a company man' – in other words, he would never side with the bullies in the team, but he would never stamp out their influence either. In that way, Cook was diplomatic rather than divisive. Was it enough for a captain to take authority on the field but let Prior and Co. get away with the behind-the-scenes sniping they apparently indulged in? It's hard to get away from the feeling that Cook was a bit too hands-off in these matters.

Cook has never gone anywhere near social media, which would have undoubtedly helped him concentrate much better on his job. It did mean he could justifiably worry what on earth the fuss was about when a parody Twitter account called @kpgenius, managed by a friend of Stuart Broad's, regularly poked fun at Pietersen during the difficult summer of 2012. This was the period around when Pietersen found himself serving a one-match ban for the text-messaging scandal. Pietersen's book claimed two things: firstly that some England players had access to the @kpgenius log-in details, and secondly that Cook, during the process in which he was helping Pietersen become reintegrated into the side, simply refused to accept that the Twitter account was an example of the bullying culture within the side.

'Cooky refused to believe the Twitter stuff. That was his way of dealing with it. It was as if he still writes to Santa Claus and puts his tooth under his pillow for the tooth fairy. Even now, he will say that he does not believe it happened.' For Pietersen, Twitter was clearly deadly serious and he clearly felt irked that Cook was above such things.

As English cricket continued its rollercoaster journey under Cook and Moores during 2014 and beyond, the captain himself was reluctant to discuss the affair. He did give an interview to the BBC in October 2014, a few days after Pietersen's autobiography had appeared. This came at a time when sentiment was cranked up to the max against the establishment and in favour of Pietersen, who had been given command of the airwaves and newspaper columns as he promoted his book.

Asked by reporter Joe Wilson if he felt 'personally hurt' by the Pietersen allegations, Cook replied: 'Yes, I do, I do, because I'm very proud of that era – to win three Ashes, become the best side in the world and play with some great players and I really only have fond memories of it, and to play under Andrew Strauss and under Andy Flower ... I only have respect for these kind of guys and I feel that era has kind of been tarnished and I'm sad about that.'

Asked to respond to the claims of a 'culture of bullying', he said: 'International cricket is a tough place and as a team you're striving for excellence at all times. At some stages those frustrations boiled over more than they should have done but only because people were desperate to succeed and wanting to know that the other ten blokes around them were 100 per cent committed to it. Did it overstep the mark a couple of times? Possibly, but we address those issues – that's what always happens in teams. It certainly wasn't a bullying environment at all in my eyes.'

However, it took Cook another four years to open up fully on the issue, in the aftermath of his own retirement, when he knew he no longer had any contractual bindings to the ECB. This time there were regrets, plus, crucially, the revelation that he had suggested a less permanent arrangement, one that gave Pietersen a chance to return to the side.

Cook said: 'I was involved in the decision at first, but the England captain doesn't have the final say on hiring and firing. I agreed with it, but I said, "Why don't we give him some time off? We can go away and maybe KP can come back later on."

'Paul Downton wanted clarity, a clean break, because people would always be asking, "When is he coming back?" You had to back his decisions because that's what his job was. The fallout was pretty nasty and I don't think the ECB handled it well or appreciated how social media worked very well then. I bore a lot of the brunt of it. I would refute anyone saying that I was the one that chucked him down the stairs, but I was involved in the decision and I believed it was right at that time. Looking back, I can safely say all the decisions I made were done for the best of the England cricket team at that time. On that one, there were a lot of other people, way above my head, also involved in it. I felt like I was being left alone as the captain.

'I haven't spoken to [Pietersen] since that day, but I think time is a great healer. We spent a lot of time together and created some amazing memories. The thing is, we never fell out. Since then, the internet has fallen out for us. As two blokes, if you take cricket out of it, we have never fallen out. He will have a different opinion, I'm sure.'

The truth boiled down to this: Cook found it no easier than a number of England players, coaches and administrators to get on with Pietersen on a daily basis. However, he did not build up a pile of resentment against him and use that resentment to goad the other man in the way that it appeared others had done. Nor would he have acted with so much finality in February 2014 if the Pietersen issue had been left entirely to him.

The first Test series in the second Moores era, which could also be called the post-Pietersen post-Swann post-Trott era, pitted England at home against Sri Lanka in two Test matches in June. There had been an unusually long five-month gap since the Ashes debacle but there had been plenty of limited-overs cricket and not all of it was good. For instance, England were bowled out for eighty-eight by the Netherlands in the World Twenty20 in Bangladesh, unbelievably. Cook was not involved in that particular fiasco.

Stumbling from one calamity to another, they also lost that home series against Sri Lanka. At Lord's, Sri Lanka's last wicket pairing clung on for a draw; in Leeds the boot was on the other foot and this time it was England's number eleven, Anderson, striving to bat out the draw with Moeen Ali. Dear old Jimmy blocked fifty-five balls and then fended off a nasty delivery from Shaminda Eranga to short leg. He only had to get through that ball, and one more, to seal the draw.

Suddenly, people were queuing up to get on Cook's case. Shane Warne, using his column in the *Daily Telegraph* (as well as the copious airtime afforded him thanks to his column), persistently attacked his captaincy style, which he had decided was both boring and negative. 'Something needs to be done,' said Cook, spikily, at one point on radio, suggesting it might be possible to muzzle the villainous Australian. Some forlorn hope that would be.

Martin Crowe, the former New Zealand batsman, opined that Cook should be ignoring the baiting from Warne and Co., although he did a bit of it himself by noting Cook the batsman had lost confidence – looking to get on to the back foot too often, looking to play square of the wicket too often. He noted a new exaggerated trigger movement, stepping back in the crease with a high backlift, was counterintuitively stopping him from playing effectively off the back foot, while also cramping his scope to meet the half-volley with a full flow of a front-foot drive down the ground.

England were having a bad time in all formats of the game, and their captain's poor form continued into the first Test against India, as Cook was bowled off his pads for just five, having spent the whole of his short innings getting too far over to the off-side trying to push the ball on to the leg side.

When India won the second Test at Lord's, a serious crisis was building. Cook could barely buy a run and the team had now gone ten Tests without a win, losing seven of them. More people queued up to question Cook. Michael Vaughan said on *Test Match Special*: 'It is probably the right thing for him to be taken away from the England captaincy. Eoin Morgan has fresh eyes, a new approach. It can't be any worse. A real decision needs to be made about Alastair Cook. I look at the way he's played – he's not scored a hundred in twenty-seven innings. Tactically, he's been all at sea for a while now. Go and spend four or five months away from cricket. He's twenty-nine years of age, he's been in this environment for eight years non-stop. That takes its toll as a player, never mind with the captaincy burden as well.'

Cook admitted himself that he now had to sort out his batting, at the very least. In a candid discussion with reporters after the Lord's Test, he said: 'If I'm not scoring runs by the end of the series and we're losing more games, it becomes tougher and tougher. Clearly I'm not the man to turn it around. Everyone has doubts. When things aren't going well, of course you have your doubts. When I was made England captain I said to my wife that I was going to give it my all. If it's not meant to be, it's not meant to be – but I want to be proud of the way I have gone about it.

'I believe the team needs me to lead them through this tough time. But if it gets to the stage where I am not scoring runs by the end of the series my position is untenable. To quit now in the middle of the series would be wrong. I'm not quitting at the moment. I've got an inner steel, which I've got to keep drawing on. First of all I've got to start scoring runs – a lot of things can change quickly from there. I hit the ball better here. I've got to back myself that a score will come. The recent past hasn't been kind to me, but we have won games with me as captain and I've won a lot of one-day games as well.'

He was not afraid to direct criticism at his own players either. 'A lot of the standout performances have been by the younger players, which is great the way they're handling Test cricket. The older guys aren't playing as well as their records suggest and that's hurting us. To win games of cricket we need at least nine or ten people playing really well. It's not happening for those guys at the moment, they've got to look at themselves. I've got to start scoring runs as well, and that can only happen with a lot of hard work.'

Moores, as ever, was positive, insisting: 'He is not hiding. He knows it is tough up here. Often under pressure he is at his best.'

Fortunately, this home Test series against India was a nice, old-fashioned, long five-Test series. If Cook and England needed it, that meant another fifteen days of cricket to turn things around.

What transpired was that they turned it round, and then some. England won at the Rose Bowl by 266 runs, they won at Old Trafford by an innings and 54 runs, and they hammered a suddenly clueless India once more, at the Oval, by an innings and 244 runs.

Cook was now entitled to laugh in the face of his fiercest critics after engineering such a dramatic turnaround in fortunes for the team. Instead, he revealed how his wife Alice had persuaded him to reverse a decision to resign the captaincy after the fourth day of the Test they had lost to Sri Lanka earlier in that strange summer.

'Without my wife, I don't think I'd be standing here as captain. You can bare your soul quite often to Alice, and she's very good at getting me back on the straight and narrow,' said Cook.

He went on to talk about character traits that have been chronicled in some detail in this book. 'I'm quite stubborn. I believe in my ability, and I'm quite a resilient guy. And that was when I needed it most. I'm glad I stuck through the tough times. That's what sport does, tests your character – and to bounce back as a team is a testament to us. I'm here because I believe that I am the right man to try to lead this team forward. I'm very, very privileged to be England captain. It's a great job to have. I'm not going to be gloating; that's not who I am. I still think I'm a fair way off my best with my batting. Until I score that hundred, everyone will always talk about it.'

Two things to pick up on here. That famous Cook stubbornness, which allowed him to play so many huge innings, impinged quite strongly on the strategic side of his captaincy, and not always in a good way. When England were striving to make things happen in games where the balance of power was tilting away from them, Cook was not always particularly good at innovating. There could, at times, be a numbing predictability about how the game would be played out, about who would be bowling at any one point and where the fielders would be positioned. Sometimes, his unyielding faith in his own judgement came up trumps. Remember when he posted himself as the solitary slip in the Ashes Test the previous year at Nottingham? It seemed a dangerous tactic, and yet it worked brilliantly.

There was also Cook's batting. He was still not quite back in the groove but he was going a lot better now, with scores of 95, 70 not out, 17 and 79 in the three Tests England won at the end of the 2014 season. The next century would surely come soon.

CHAPTER SEVENTEEN

MAJOR SERIES SUCCESSES

From 2015 onwards, Alastair Cook's mind was no longer cluttered with the additional baggage of leading England's one-day side. He did not take news of his sacking at all well, though it was pretty inevitable – his form completely dropped off in the ODI format in a seven-match series in Sri Lanka which England lost 5-2. It did not particularly help that Downton kept on insisting Cook was the right man to lead England into the World Cup before then yanking the rug from under him.

Refreshed and concentrating on Test cricket alone – with a few extra opportunities to play for his long-lost county, Essex, to factor in too – Cook led England on a three-match tour of the Caribbean in the spring of 2015, a series that was shared 1-1. The winning thread was still not recaptured when New Zealand dropped by for two more Tests in late May, but at least Cook was now hitting top form with the bat again. He scored two centuries and three fifties in the first five Tests of 2015, coming into form nicely, it seemed, for another crack at the Aussies. This was an extraordinarily important series for Cook, personally, and England, spiritually. The gulf between the administrators and the fans had never been so big. Supporters who had once been proud to wear the Barmy Army T-shirt, or buy their children those lurid blue polyester one-day shirts, still really resented being described as existing in a world 'outside cricket'.

England had been bundled out of the World Cup embarrassingly early in the spring to extend a run of miserable and unmitigated failure in the tournament. Yet if there is one thing, even more than a World Cup, that can put a spring back in the steps of England supporters, it is a successful Ashes campaign.

Sparks of a revival, ideologically at least, came in some vibrant displays in 50-over cricket. Peter Moores had quietly been sacked for a second time and England let their hair down with the bat in a home ODI series against one of the World Cup finalists, New Zealand, winning it 3-2 on the back of some huge totals.

That, however, was under the captaincy of Eoin Morgan. It was now time for Cook to deliver something similar in the Test environment and not everyone thought he would be able to do that. He was losing support in some notable quarters too, with Geoffrey Boycott, who frequently described Cook as 'not a great captain' on *Test Match Special*, losing his temper in his *Daily Telegraph* column. After a fairly mild slur about the characteristics of Yorkshiremen by the England captain, Boycott responded fiercely: 'Alastair is so up his own arse, he thinks he is untouchable as captain. He acts as if he is the best captain England have ever had, comparable with Jardine, Hutton, Illingworth and Vaughan. He is living in cloud cuckoo land about his captaincy ability.'

England began the Ashes as underdogs with the bookmakers, despite the late retirement through injury of the paceman Ryan Harris. In Australia, Ladbrokes gave the visitors a 72 per cent chance of winning the series. The history of sport is well chronicled with underdog triumphs, however, and this turned out to be another. In the opener at Cardiff, Joe Root was tremendous with the bat while extra bowling options in the era of multiple England all-rounders like Moeen Ali and Ben Stokes meant Anderson and Broad could bowl shorter, sharper spells. England won easily in Cardiff, and though Australia produced a powerhouse display to level it up at Lord's, Anderson and Steven Finn bowled superbly well on a sportier wicket at Edgbaston as England nosed in front again. The series was effectively sealed on the first morning of the fourth Test at Trent Bridge when Stuart Broad took 8-15 in Australia's 60 all out. The Aussies whinged about the ball swinging too much, but the reality is that while they were improving rapidly in non-English conditions their techniques did not adapt well to coping with lateral movement.

While not a classic Ashes series by any means, it was one of extraordinary fulfilment for Cook, who lost what seemed a critical toss in the all-important third Test at Edgbaston and yet did everything right in the field to help ensure Australia were bowled out for 136. At Trent Bridge, he took the right gamble, putting the Aussies in and watching as Broad did the rest. The excellent blogger Jarrod Kimber noted: 'There was a time when Cook's captaincy was essentially batting and walking out on the field. It was dour, harder to watch than even his scratchiest innings. But as his team changed, he stopped being Andrew Strauss lite, started to grow into the job. He had funky third slips in helmets, he attacked more and he changed when he had to. Alastair Cook is a man who works hard on his craft.'

It was a series when Cook did most things right, and learned to improvise a little, as hard as it might have been to somebody who preferred to play the notes on the page. At Lord's, he put himself in the unusual position of short mid-on and took a catch to end a dangerous innings from Steve Smith. On the fourth day, he brought Moeen back into the attack just before lunch to try to get rid of David Warner. It was a bold move because Warner had thrashed Moeen merrily a little earlier, but this time Moeen had his revenge and got the fast-scoring left-hander lbw.

After the Trent Bridge Test, Cook allowed his emotions to wash over him, his voice catching and tears welling up, though he insisted the reaction was triggered not by his own feelings of relief and joy but by the announcement – made then and there – that his opposite number Michael Clarke had decided to retire.

'Michael's got emotional and it's got me emotional,' said Cook. 'From where we've been over the last eighteen months to what we've achieved, I'm incredibly proud of the lads and all the support staff. We've done something I didn't think was quite possible at the beginning of the summer. When you lose 5-0, there's a turnover of players and a new side develops, it takes a bit of time but you see what talent there is in the country and we saw the end potential here. Today's not about me, or me getting emotional – it's about players who have taken that journey through some incredibly tough times to get the amazing times.'

Cook had led England to six Ashes Test successes, behind only Mike Brearley (eleven) and W.G. Grace (eight), and although England's momentum was checked by another defeat in the UAE to Pakistan, it was a series that featured 450 runs from the bat of Cook across five innings, including another of his monster scores, a 263. No other England batsman made a single century.

When Cook's batting reached a low point at the end of the previous year, he sought out a batting coach called Gary Palmer, an all-rounder who had played for Somerset in the 1980s, but usually only when the likes of Ian Botham and Viv Richards weren't available. Palmer was not well known around the England scene, but Gooch suggested to Cook that it might be a good idea to get some input from someone with a fresh perspective. Cook was ushered in for private sessions, driving to and from Palmer's Oxfordshire academy, and when he was next seen adopting a more open stance to stop him falling away to the off-side, it transpired that this was a direct product of Palmer's involvement. Cook was better balanced and well positioned to follow through the line of the ball more cleanly.

He was also content to be working with new coaches Paul Farbrace and Trevor Bayliss in the England set-up, though he was even happier that the national team structure was now headed by his old opening partner, Andrew Strauss.

The next examination of Cook's combined abilities as captain and batsman came with the first tour of South Africa since 2009–10. This turned out to be another very impressive triumph. Just like in the previous summer's Ashes, none of the matches were close as England consistently put up good totals with Ben Stokes, Joe Root and Jonny Bairstow all hitting at least one century and one half-century each. Stuart Broad, on the form of his life, took eighteen wickets across the four Tests at an average of 20.61, and England clinched the series with a game to spare.

George Dobell summed up Cook's collective achievements by telling Cricinfo readers: 'Cook is the only man in history to lead his side to Test series victories in India and South Africa. When you add in a couple of Ashes wins, you have what has become – despite all the criticism – a deeply impressive track record. History may reflect on Cook, as a batsman and a leader, and wonder what all the fuss was about.'

At Johannesburg's Wanderers ground, he persisted with Stuart Broad in the second innings after the bowler, for the second time in the match, had started unimpressively. He was handsomely rewarded as Broad scythed through the South African batting and simultaneously saw James Taylor take a couple of fine catches positioned at an unusually deep short leg.

South Africa were, at this time, the highest-ranked side in Test cricket, so to beat them overseas was a significant achievement. Even if England's failure to beat lesser sides like New Zealand and West Indies meant they were not threatening to take over the mantle, it was much sweeter for the supporters to see them excel against the really good teams.

Having said that, it was encouraging for England to win their first home series of 2016, against Sri Lanka, 2-0. There followed a surprise defeat to Pakistan at Lord's in mid-July, a match which was the tenth in succession without a Cook century. In fact, for seventeen consecutive Tests he had produced just one hundred, that huge 263 in Abu Dhabi. Once a world leader in converting fifties, he was now getting stuck too often between forty and ninety-nine.

One of the problems Cook now had to deal with was the persistent absence of a settled opening partner. In the post-Strauss era, Nick Compton, Michael Carberry and Sam Robson had come and gone. Joe Root and Moeen Ali had been promoted up from the middle order and then shifted back to where they belonged. Even Jonathan Trott had made an aborted attempt to resume his Test career at the top of the order. Adam Lyth was the latest man to be trialled and discarded, and the current incumbent was Alex Hales, more naturally suited to white-ball cricket where he was enjoying plenty of success in England colours.

What this really underlined, apart from anything else, was how hard it has always been for an opening batsman to excel in Test cricket. It also put into very sharp focus what Cook had achieved and how England might struggle once he had decided enough was finally enough. He was still only thirty-one, and retirement did not seem a likely prospect at the moment, nor did an end to his captaincy. The crisis in confidence on that front had been quelled, for the time being, in 2014 when England got over their Headingley mishap against Sri Lanka by crushing India.

Cook needed a century and England needed a response to the Lord's defeat against Pakistan. On the first day at Old Trafford it all came together. Cook hit 105 in a first-day score of 314-4.

The twenty-ninth Test century had taken some time coming and, unusually, he got there in less than four hours, the second fifty coming at virtually a run a ball. It was a Cook hundred that summed up Cook the batsman: survival against the new ball, a measured fifty with a reliance on his most loyal weapon, the cut shot, for boundaries and a more expansive move towards the century with some really excellent hitting straight down the ground. There were times in Cook's career when he was simply unable to hit the ball back past the bowler. Since seeing Palmer, he found the shot much easier.

England won at Old Trafford very easily. There was some annoyance that Cook did not enforce the follow-on when Pakistan were bowled out more than 350 runs behind, but both Anderson and Broad were in their thirties now and the captain had to be mindful of managing their workload at all times. England also won comfortably at Edgbaston, whereupon they only needed a draw at the Oval, often a good venue to try to find one, to win the series. Pakistan's fast bowlers struck gold on the first morning, however, and it needed runs down the order to take England to 328. When Pakistan responded with 542, featuring 218 from Younis Khan, they had seized control and went on to record a ten-wicket win.

Afterwards, Cook highlighted concerns with England's batting that, to this day, remain unaddressed. There simply seems to be a shocking dearth of specialist batsmen coming through the counties. In that series against Pakistan in 2016, Hales, James Vince and Gary Ballance all proved to be significant disappointments. England's most recent Test, against West Indies, featured a top three of Rory Burns, Keaton Jennings and Joe Denly, all of whom are making their way in international cricket, Denly at the age of thirty-three.

It can only be an anecdotal view, but I am strongly of the opinion that more and more of the most gifted potential players in England are being lost to cricket at an alarmingly young age. There has never been a time when there are so many different sports as well as non-sporting activities for youngsters to do, and where once cricket had a special place as the nation's semi-official summer sport, now it exists on the same playing field as so many others. By having a short season that correlates to only one academic term in Britain – and that term being one that often features major exams – cricket is further excluded. The drop-off in sixteen-year-olds playing the sport is dramatic.

My fifteen-year-old son has played six seasons of Colts Cricket at a club on the outskirts of north London. Whereas initially the three age groups were oversubscribed to the extent that competition for places in the teams was fierce, now they are desperately scrabbling to find eleven players simply to make up a team. In one fixture last year, a rival team turned up with only eight players. Two clubs in the same regional division with fine facilities have been extremely successful at recruiting and can produce two teams per age group, but at the other clubs the interest is dwindling rapidly. This is borne out in cold, hard statistics. The figures show that around a quarter of a million people in the UK play cricket, about half of what it was twenty years ago.

You may ask, what has this got to do with Alastair Cook? The fact is, there isn't a direct connection. I simply find it something of a sadness that his remarkable career has coincided with a time in which cricket has gradually declined as an influence within British culture. For all the blood, sweat and tears expended by Cook in his long career, there is little to show for it in terms of a legacy of engagement.

A rather large share of the blame for this can be directly laid at the door of the England and Wales Cricket Board. It has consistently sold out to the highest bidders, Sky and now BT Sport, for TV rights, without taking into account that cricket would become an unconsidered pastime for a generation of children with parents who did not already have an interest in the sport.

The ECB would say that receiving more money from Sky and BT Sport has allowed them to invest more heavily in the grass roots of the game. There is no evidence for this. Many club grounds have poor facilities, barely usable nets, a part-time groundsman (if they're lucky), and the majority of the coaches are parent volunteers. I have enquired within clubs about this mythical uplift in 'grass-roots funding' and they tell me there is none.

You may have already heard this tale of lament a few times already. In 1999, Derek Birley wrote in *A Social History of English Cricket*: 'It is to be hoped that amid all the excitements of reorganising the first-class game, the ECB do not lose sight of the need to give high priority to attracting youngsters into cricket ... by addressing the long-neglected problems in school and local clubs and providing decent playing surfaces and team equipment. In a country awash with lottery money it should not be too difficult. And, difficult or not, it is absolutely vital to the health of the game. Cricket was originally a schoolboy game, and is still mainly learned at school. It is not the sort of game that is easily learned in adult life. Nor are adult spectators likely to take to it if they have to learn from scratch a whole set of elaborate rules and conventions, and to appreciate sophisticated batting and bowling techniques.'

The worrying thing is that twenty years on the situation is no better, even though some are keen to help. Jeremy Farrell, Cook's cricket master at Bedford, wishes he could find a way of opening up the facilities at his current school, Sutton Valence, to other local children who are not fortunate enough to have parents who can afford school fees.

'I do worry about the grass roots because I always saw it as my responsibility to provide not only Test cricketers, but also the club Second XI stalwarts who make cricket what it is on a local level. My dad would play club cricket all the way through the summer. We need to make sure the concept of a player who commits to playing for his local club all through the summer continues.

'I would love more children to have a chance to use our facilities. We've got the appetite and space for it. All we need is somebody to help get those children here and back again, a few volunteers. There are always swathes of time when our facilities are lying dormant and we would love to find a way – it boils down to logistics.' It boils down to volunteers, really. The grimmest scenario of all is that when the current generation of schoolkids become parents the numbers of volunteers will also drop off sharply.

Ronnie Irani, Cook's first professional captain at Essex, remembers during the summer of 2005 driving past a suburban garden and seeing a sight he had not seen before. Remember, this was the last year Test cricket was shown live on free-to-air television in Britain.

Irani recalls: 'The daughter was batting, mum was at slip, one brother was bowling and another fielding. They didn't have the latest bat and they were using the dog's tennis ball, but they were playing cricket because England had that love for the game.

I didn't see a satellite dish on the side of the house. That summer, everyone was playing cricket – on the street, in their front garden – I have not seen that since then. The game's definitely suffered.'

CHAPTER EIGHTEEN

RETURNING TO ESSEX

Bangladesh still lose the majority of their games but have come a long way since their introduction into Test cricket in 2000. At home they have the ability to produce either dour, slow pitches or ones that gradually deteriorate and can become very awkward to bat on. In that scenario it's hard for them to win Tests, especially when their opponents are batting last. In the first of two Tests they hosted against Alastair Cook's England in the autumn of 2016, they came very close to winning, only to fall twenty-three runs short of their victory target when Ben Stokes summoned up a final burst of energy to trap numbers ten and eleven lbw in the space of three balls. It was to be the last England Test victory with Cook as captain.

Bangladesh were less charitable in the second match, and this time it was England who had to bat last, chasing an awkward 273. When Cook and Ben Duckett, yet another new batting partner, found the first hundred of those runs without being parted everything looked hunky-dory. Once Duckett was dismissed, England collapsed in a sea of panic and got nowhere near their victory target.

Succumbing so meekly against Bangladesh was no sort of preparation for the upcoming tour of India featuring five Tests. The home side won emphatically by a 4-0 margin, doing so despite Cook winning the toss four times. In the fourth Test in Mohali, England scored 400 in the first innings and lost. In the closing match in Chennai, they put up 477 and still lost. The final-day collapse carried powerful echoes of what had happened in Bangladesh a couple of months earlier.

Had the time finally come for Cook to check out of Test match captaincy? Indeed it had. In February 2017, he announced his resignation at the age of thirty-two. He had stepped to the middle fifty-nine times to toss a small coin by a twenty-two-yard mown strip with a rival Test captain. Now it was time to let somebody else do that job and perhaps overhaul his own English record for captaincy appearances.

Cook won 41 per cent of his Tests as captain, a poorer win percentage than Michael Vaughan, Peter May or Andrew Strauss among those England skippers to lead their country in more than forty Tests. Yet he had won four big series – two away series in India and South Africa, and two home Ashes Test series. Only one of those four successes came with England favourites to win.

England and Wales Cricket Board director of cricket Andrew Strauss, Cook's predecessor as captain, said his former opening partner was owed 'a great debt of gratitude' by his country. Strauss said: 'He's led the team with determination, conviction and a huge amount of pride over the last five years and his record stands for itself. He deserves to be seen as one of our country's great captains.'

There remained, of course, plenty of unfinished business for Cook the player, particularly in an England shirt, but also for his county. The summer of 2017 featured no Test cricket until July, with England hosting the Champions Trophy. What that meant was that Cook was available for Essex for considerably more time than he had been for more than a decade. With more than half of the County Championship matches also scheduled for that opening tranche of the season, it meant Cook was able to play in seven of Essex's first eight Championship matches and his runs contributed significantly to the county making a fast start in the competition with four wins and three draws in those matches.

After playing in all seven summer Tests, first against South Africa and then West Indies, Cook had hoped to go back to

Essex for at least one more match to help them lift their first Championship pennant since 1992, in their first season since being promoted from Division Two, but was ordered to rest up by England coach Trevor Bayliss ahead of the Ashes tour.

Nevertheless, his stint earlier in the season had produced 667 runs from 10 innings with a high score of 193, and two other centuries. His enthusiasm for the county that had nurtured him, but which he had largely been forced to abandon from a very young age given the demands placed on him by an England contract, still sparkled. Indeed, it still sparkles even now as he has signed a deal to keep him playing at Essex until 2021. Yes, you really can pay a few quid to see a knight of the realm marching out of that functional 1970s pavilion in Chelmsford day after day through the summer months for the next two and a half years.

Irani says: 'He loves cricket, genuinely loves the game. He loves batting and batting and batting, catching the odd ball at slip, then back to batting again. Essex lost him at quite an early age. We helped with his development but he achieved it himself, but we got involved with him and then we lost him to England. So it was a massive blow for us. So to have him coming back and doing what he's doing is wonderful. I wish a lot more top cricketers had more respect for county cricket; maybe that would have a positive knock-on effect on other key stakeholders at ECB. Maybe they should think about it. Hang on a minute, Alastair Cook is going back to playing county cricket, now why is that? This brand, county cricket, is 130 years old and is one of the iconic brands of the world. What do we do with it?'

The frequently and often justifiably maligned ECB have mucked about so much with the county calendar that one year's fixture list never remotely corresponds to the previous one. They have often pushed much of the County Championship into spring and autumn slots and they often seem to deliberately avoid weekends and bank holidays for some perplexing reason, forcing most people below retirement age to take days off work to watch games. They invented Twenty20 cricket but made no effort to market it to global TV audiences or even the global talent pool of players, and it became a penalty kick for other leagues around the world (notably India) to pick it up and turn it into the huge cash cow it now is. The latest idea, one the ECB has been plotting long and hard over, is The Hundred – a hundred-ball-a-side league in which the eighteen counties will be distilled into eight 'city-based franchises', a depressing prospect indeed and one that would tear the soul out of the existing first-class structure.

Ronnie Irani is among those who are frustrated that the ECB has neglected the history of the domestic game while desperately, and belatedly, trying to cash in on the short format. He says: 'There is one country in the world which sells out in Test cricket and that's England. I just wish that the ECB had invested in the county game. County cricket is tribal, you still have the county you're proud of. If you're a Yorkshireman you support Yorkshire cricket, you don't support Leeds cricket. If you're Sheffield are you going to support Leeds? With the amount of money that comes into the game they could have done something with the counties and really upped the ante. County cricket is one of the greatest brands in the world of sport and we do nothing about it. Grass-roots cricketers, those who don't make it for their county, are potentially grass-roots supporters of the game and we don't look at that from an ECB perspective.

'There is too much history and background for us to be talking about the death of county cricket. All it needs is someone with a bit about them, who loves the game of cricket, to invest in it. You go to any Test country of the world and ask the players there, "Would you like to play county cricket one day?" I guarantee the answers is yes.'

CHAPTER NINETEEN

THE PERFECT SEND-OFF

A lastair Cook played twenty-one Tests back in the ranks as a player under the captaincy of Joe Root before retiring from international cricket altogether. In the first two series, at home to South Africa and West Indies, England performed strongly to take both rubbers and convince the selectors that Root was the right man for the job. Cook was not getting as many centuries as he had in his prime, but still had the wherewithal to hit the odd really big score. He was under absolutely no pressure for his place, considering England's general top-order malaise and persistent reliance on the lower order to bail out the specialist batsmen. He struck 243 against West Indies at Edgbaston as a more-than-gentle reminder that he still had the scope, hunger, and reserves of concentration to put a game out of reach of an opposing side if everything fell into place.

In Cook's final Ashes tour, England were regrettably taken to the cleaners once again. It was not quite a 5-0 pasting to match those miserable series in Australia that Cook had known only too well (2006–07 and 2013–14) but it was a painful time for Root's squad all the same. It was almost poignant that the one game England were able to save was the one in which Cook compiled his last great masterpiece, a ten-and-a-half hour 244 in which he carried his bat. He did not even reach forty in any of his other innings in Australia as various technical issues began to eat away at him again, but for that one knock at Melbourne, everything was just so right. On a good wicket he was able to meet the ball at the top of the bounce and punch it down the ground or off the back foot for boundaries. Dropped on slip at sixty-six, and once more on 153, he nevertheless timed the ball pleasingly and the longer he batted the more assured his footwork became. Driving cleanly in the 'V' and dispatching the short stuff, he continued to keep an on-form Australian attack at bay and the Barmy Army roared its delight as he drove Jackson Bird handsomely straight past the umpire to record his fifth and final double hundred. Meeting Cook in Sydney before the final Ashes Test, Jeremy Farrell remembers the ex-England captain telling him that he'd had a training session that morning. 'He always used to talk about practice. There's a subtle difference between practice and training. Training is a bit of a burden; practice is about how you are going to get better. I certainly didn't have a tip-off he was about to retire when he did but, in hindsight, that little conversation in Sydney revealed quite a lot.'

Though Cook showed he could make the odd 200-plus score in this period, he was really struggling to do much else. Since the 243 at Edgbaston in August, he had gone ten innings without a half-century and then made the Melbourne 244. He dropped into poor form again after that innings, a run that took in two Tests in New Zealand in which his top score in four innings was just fourteen, England losing the series 1-0. Either exhibiting an alarming lack of footwork or dangling the bat outside off stump uncertainly, he suddenly looked as vulnerable as he ever had done. Bowlers were allowed to bowl well at him, as Trent Boult did in the first innings at Auckland, but the other three dismissals in New Zealand were avoidable.

Cook's rocky form continued in England's home season in 2018 and a quandary seemed to be brewing now. Would it be easier, at some point, for England to rebuild the side without Alastair Cook? In other words, would two opening batsmen find life easier, rather than one who would simply be regarded as 'Cook's latest partner' and drink from what appeared to be, if not a poisoned chalice, then at least a cursed one?

Root's England did not initially respond convincingly to the poor tour of the Antipodean nations, losing the first Test against Pakistan at Lord's. They began to thread things together, however, to beat those opponents at Leeds and then move 2-1 up in the five-match series against India as the teams moved to the Rose Bowl.

Cook's Melbourne masterpiece now seemed a distant memory. Although he had started the summer with a nice 70 against Pakistan at Lord's, he then went 1, 46, 13, 0, 21, 29 and 17.

'There is an issue,' Mike Atherton told viewers on Sky Sports. 'Cook himself is not old in terms of years, but is quite old in terms of the games he has played. At the top of the order, facing the best bowlers in the world, I know what it is like and it will get to you in the end. Cook is very inconsistent at the moment, feast or famine.'

As England and India headed to the Rose Bowl for the fourth Test, Will Macpherson, in the *Evening Standard*, was hoping Cook's excellent record at Hampshire's modern and peculiarly located ground might help him come good.

Macpherson wrote: 'A career as long as Cook's – this will be his 158th successive Test – has its peaks and troughs. He saved it once with a second innings century at the Oval against Pakistan in 2010, and again at Southampton in 2014. This form slump is peculiar as he has been looking fluent then getting out. He would love India to leave out Ishant Sharma and Ravi Ashwin. They will not oblige: both bowl beautifully to him. There is a school of thought that Cook has earned the right to leave Test cricket on his own terms, and that he can simply decide when he finishes. This is not true; Kevin Pietersen and Ian Bell, both of whom he played more than a hundred Tests with, did not get that luxury, and nor did Cook in one-day cricket. He knows that if he wants to continue, he must be worth his spot in the side.'

Meanwhile, the support from within the camp was vehement. 'I actually like it when you write him off because every time he's written off he comes back with a double hundred,' said Root.

Returns of seventeen and twelve at the Rose Bowl were inadequate, and England's whole top order imploded horribly on the first day when they were 86-6 at one stage. Sam Curran with the bat and Moeen Ali with the ball then lifted England to a position approaching parity before yet more lower-order runs in the second innings presented an awkward enough target of 245 for India. England snagged a sixty-run win and they had beaten India yet again on home soil with a match to play.

One day later came the big announcement. Cook was ready to call it quits in Test cricket. He would bow out after the final Test at the Oval, whether he scored three hundred or two ducks, whether England won, drew or lost. 'Although it is a sad day, I can retire with a big smile on my face knowing I have given everything and there is nothing left in the tank. I have achieved more than I could have ever imagined and feel very privileged to have played for such a long time alongside some of the greats of the English game. The thought of not sharing the dressing room again with some of my teammates was the hardest part of my decision, but I know the timing is right.'

While Cook's teammates splurged their appreciation on Twitter, a more considered response came from Graham Gooch. He was the man most responsible for transforming a determined but callow youngster into the finished model – a batsman who could regularly make the best bowlers in the world wilt under barrage after barrage of runs.

Gooch said: 'Alastair has been the rock of England's batting for the last twelve years and while we are all sad to see him retire, we must rejoice in what he has done for our country. He is a genuine legend of English cricket.

'He is a legend not only because of his performances, but also because of his attitude, his sacrifices, the way he has carried himself and the example he has set. Alastair is a perfect role model and is the image of the game we want to project. He is a great ambassador for his sport; he is a great person as well as a great cricketer.'

Cook could not have wished for a more welcome scenario in which to complete his farewell. This was a dead rubber with the series already won; in many ways there could not be less pressure on him to perform. Yet he must have felt a duty to go out and get runs, to sign off in style, not with a whimper. In the preliminaries, Joe Root said: 'It would seem fitting for him to go out on a high personal note. Hopefully, he can soak up everything else that comes with this week and go out and deliver on the field. It would be nice to start and finish with a century. You never know, it might be written in the stars.'

You will, presumably, have read Daniel Norcross's excellent prologue detailing the thrill of commentating on Cook's century at the Oval. It was set up by his most commanding innings in the series to date, a carefully compiled seventy-one on the opening day, an innings that was ended when he chopped a delivery on to his stumps. A huge collective sigh was heard across the famous south London ground before folk recovered their dignity, rose to their feet and applauded him back to the pavilion. Those with tickets for day three also had a chance for one of those 'I was there' moments as Cook reached forty-six in his second innings – though they probably went home wishing they could also come back the day after. On the fourth day, a Monday in September when sport would rarely impinge on the collective conscience, Test cricket held the attention, not just of the thousands in the Oval, but perhaps a few million others too, one way or another. Through the multitude of ways sport can be followed as we approach the third decade of the twenty-first century, these cricket lovers might have been nipping out for an early lunch break to catch a TV screen in a pub, or maybe tuning into radio coverage or an online video stream of questionable legality. Perhaps one of the many live text blogs would have to suffice. Cook was on ninety-six with half an hour to go until the lunch interval when Ravi Jadeja spun a ball in quite sharply from outside off stump. The batsman watched it as carefully as the other 26,485 balls he had faced in Test cricket, and steered it securely to third man for a single. Now here was a gift from the Indians; a wild throw speeding to the boundary to gift Cook an extra four runs, and there it was – the century.

Some of the national records he established were by wide margins. His final haul of 12,472 dwarfs the next best for England – Graham Gooch on 8,900. His thirty-three centuries are ten more than Kevin Pietersen's, while there were global records too. Cook was the youngest player to reach all of the one thousand-run landmarks between seven thousand and twelve thousand, and the only opener to hit more than ten thousand runs.

There is little more to add than to acknowledge his knighthood, announced in December 2018, making him that very rare thing – an active professional sportsman who should, correctly, be addressed as 'Sir'. Ian Botham had to wait until many years after he had finished playing the game to gain this level of royal approval. The rowers Steven Redgrave and Matthew Pinsent were also knighted only after retiring. When he scored a century in Essex's first match of the 2019 season against Cambridge, the Essex captain Ryan ten Doeschate made it clear that a Cook England comeback was unlikely, but remained a possibility: 'I know how much he does love England cricket and how much work he's put in there so, no, I wouldn't rule it out in times of desperation and if he was playing really well and he felt the desire was there ... I guess there's no reason why he couldn't make a comeback.' Cook himself dangled a bit of a carrot when he said a week later: 'I've played my last game for England. There's always that one thing, if there's an absolute emergency or something... But I'm nowhere near that mindset.'

So what else besides Essex? Jeremy Farrell predicts: 'He will look to spend a lot of time with his family. I think he will be at some point quite interested in coaching but not necessarily in a high-profile role, maybe in one of those roles where you just work with individual players. He loves his farming. I think it's sixteen years since he left school, so this is his sixteenth gap year. I don't know if he will ever look to do something like a university degree.'

Ronnie Irani would love to see him develop his punditry, which was heard for the first time on *Test Match Special* during the tour of the West Indies at the start of the year. 'I enjoy listening to him on the radio, but on that I am probably biased. He's got massive respect from within the game.' One issue that sits a little uncomfortably when assessing whether he can make a good objective on-air analyst is that there are players in the team who he is still a bit too close to. As Cook said in an interview in *The Sunday Times*: 'I am not going to criticise James Anderson if he has a bad day. Broady, too. There is no way around it. We have been through so much together, especially Jimmy. I have too much respect for him and I am too friendly with him.' Interestingly, he was not afraid to praise the selectors when they dropped Keaton Jennings, his final Test partner, ahead of the second Test in the West Indies. So it might just be a case of waiting for Anderson to retire and then Cook might be able to blossom as a TV or radio pundit.

I am not sure he could follow recent former players like Andrew Strauss and Ashley Giles into administration. There are certain to be some scars left behind from the grim internal dealings he had to be privy to when the issue of Kevin Pietersen was dissected ad nauseam.

His absence will be sorely felt in the next few years when England's Test team encounter the inevitable troughs that will come their way. It already is. In the first six post-Cook Tests so far, England's opening partnerships have produced on average 25.8. Rory Burns has played in all three of those Tests, but he's already had three different partners.

How long will it be until England next win a Test series in Australia or India? It could be a very long time. Unquestionably, those two England highlights in the post-2005 era would never have been achieved without Sir Alastair Cook's barrage of runs.

The first Test of this summer's Ashes will be the first that does not feature Alastair Cook since Kevin Pietersen broke Australian hearts in the barely believable 2005 series. Cook encapsulated the dogged defiance that enabled England to achieve some great things in Test cricket between 2006 and 2018. They didn't always have the best players in the world, and they certainly had to come through some low points. But they did get their hands on the number-one ranking while enjoying plenty of success against their most formidable opponents – Australia, India and South Africa.

It is time now for others to ensure Cook does not leave only memories behind. Other batsmen must have the patience to play the ten-hour innings that can define whole series. If England start to mourn the absence of Cook the record-breaking batsman, it will be because they are not learning from the quiet determination that he brought to Test-match cricket, the same quiet determination that allowed him to dominate his rivals time and time again.